Life
CAN BE A BOWL
OF BERRIES

LOG ON TO GOD

ANNE CARBONE

WESTBOW
PRESS®
A DIVISION OF THOMAS NELSON
& ZONDERVAN

WestBow Press books may be ordered through booksellers or by contacting:

WestBow Press
A Division of Thomas Nelson & Zondervan
1663 Liberty Drive
Bloomington, IN 47403
www.westbowpress.com
844-714-3454

Scripture taken from the New King James Version®. Copyright © 1982
by Thomas Nelson. Used by permission. All rights reserved.

ISBN: 978-1-6642-5237-0 (sc)
ISBN: 978-1-6642-5238-7 (hc)
ISBN: 978-1-6642-5239-4 (e)

Library of Congress Control Number: 2021924843

Print information available on the last page.

WestBow Press rev. date: 12/17/2021

Dedication

I dedicate this book to the men and women who became our heroes during the pandemic of 2020. In a time of fear, anxiety, sickness, and death, they stood courageous and fought for us. Our health-care workers, police, fire fighters, teachers, emergency services personnel, spiritual leaders—all those who stood in the trenches and fought. I salute you and honor you. I will keep you in my prayers. Thank you for all you did during this time, sacrificing family time, risking exposure, and experiencing fatigue. You witnessed death. I also must add the crews who stocked our grocery stores and pharmacies, the delivery people who brought our take-out orders and groceries, and our postal workers who brought our mail and packages. Thank you to all who played a part in the complete recovery that I hope we will see soon. Thank you. Through two world wars, the Great Depression, the tragedy of 9/11, and the 2020 pandemic, we are American strong, one nation under God.

Contents

Preface

I could hear the doctor talking as he walked toward my room. "Let's ask Annie," he said. It was a newly diagnosed condition, which meant a new medication added to my routine, a new device to monitor the medical condition at home, and maybe a need for resources available in our area. The staff always answered questions and gave information, instruction, and most of all encouragement. As part of my job for over twenty-five years, I began to think about how God gives us these same things. I became aware of little things that added to my day that were like all of the above: communication, information, and encouragement. It was sweet, and I called them berry moments. I shared those moments in a blog, and now I share them with you in *Life Can Be a Bowl of Berries*. The following pages contain postings from random thoughts, divine appointments, and wisdom from scripture, sent from our Heavenly Father to sweeten our days.

I published a book that was meant to be a medical history as well as a memoir for my grandchildren. The purpose of the blog was to answer the many questions the readers were asking and create a dialogue that would answer those questions. The blog was a journal of random thoughts and events and discussion of how they contribute to our relationship and communication with God. I have always felt a connection to God, not realizing that God was communicating with me. This book shares those random thoughts and events. I wish you many blessings and berries to you and yours.

Definition of a Berry

A berry is a small, pulpy, and edible fruit. Typically, berries are juicy, rounded, and brightly colored. They can also be sweet or tart and do not have a stone or pit, although many have pips or seeds.

Berries have been a valuable food source since before the modern agriculture. Fruit is mentioned or referred to in the Bible over sixty times. Fruit plays a part in the scriptures; for example, the Garden of Eden had apples. Archaeologists are discovering seeds and fruit that give us data and insight to ancient diets and agriculture. The colors of fruits are used to describe cars, makeup, nail polish, paint colors, and clothing. Crimson, pomegranate, and apple red are some that come to mind. Last, and most important to our health, berries are filled with nutrients that benefit us. They are loaded with antioxidants, keeping free radicals under control. They are also high in fiber and help fight inflammation. Studies have shown they may help to relieve stress and maintain good blood-sugar levels. They are good for our health. When a sweet little thing occurs in your activities of daily living, consider it a berry for your spirit—an encouragement, direction, and message from heaven and a good thing for the body and soul. I wish you a bowlful of berries every day.

Oh, taste and see that the Lord is good; blessed is the man who trusts in Him! (Psalm 34:8)

Acknowledgments

Without the support from my family and friends, this book would have not come to fruition. Their prayers and encouragement brightened my spirit. On the days I thought I could not deal with one more computer glitch, they were there with the right words and the answer. My limited knowledge on how to navigate the digital world was at times overwhelming. That's when my bright, intelligent, computer-savvy grandson came to help. Thank you, Michael, for the amount of time taken out of your busy life to help me get this book into print. *Thank you* falls short of expressing my gratitude for your help. Thank you, Holy Spirit, for your guidance on the dark days. Thank you, Jesus, for allowing me to share what you have done in my life and will do for others.

Introduction

I was teaching a class in my home after school for third- and fourth-grade children to prepare them to give their first confession of sins to the priest. Our lessons focused on sins, forgiveness of sins, and the proper protocol upon entering the confessional. What I was getting back from my students was fear, shame, and a lot of questions about sin. I felt ineffective as a teacher because I had no answers. I searched the material given to me to teach each lesson and still found no answers. We had no Bibles available, so I went to the library and found one. What I discovered was a loving God who forgives freely. I found a loving God waiting for His flock to come home and find Him. Forgiveness can happen with a conversation with God anytime, anyplace. I could not stop reading. I was able to speak to my students about living lives with no shame or fear and share a loving God with them. Using the Ten Commandments as a guide for future decisions, we defined *sin*. Our art project was a scroll of the Ten Commandments. That was more than thirty years ago. I never taught that class again, but I am still walking on that amazing path of discovery of Jesus Christ. Find Jesus in the everyday and become aware of how He can speak to you. He found me in the library and spoke to me there.

Author's Note

I wrote this book because I was excited to share how God speaks. It took some time for me to put it all together and realize He was speaking. I pray it comes sooner for you. He speaks in nature, in that still small voice, and in the reading of the Bible as that word pops off the page just for you and the situation you are facing. He speaks in everyday events, random thoughts, and divine appointments. This book shares some of those moments of revelation, comfort, and teaching that occurred in my life. May the book help you define these sweet moments I call berry moments. As a mother, grandmother, nurse, missionary, and mentor, I have witnessed a bunch of berries, although sometimes I did not recognize them right away. Some berries have to ripen before you get the full flavor of the sweetness. May you experience many berries and feel peace in the storm.

Trials are meant for growth and maturity, not death. Revelation comes in dark places, and power comes from survival. Joy is not achieved through external things. The moment you whisper the words *thank you*, your intimate relationship with God begins. The situation that caused that whisper created the divine appointment for you to go deeper with Jesus. May this book help you begin to recognize the sweet things that God allows to come into your life, the berry moments. Incidentally, I lived on Berry Street as a child. Please email me at bowlofberries101@gmail.com if you want to share your berries.

1

ALIGNMENT NEEDED

I was watering my vegetables and plants one day when a spray of water launched out of the hose connection. My daughter had helped me fix it a few weeks earlier; with her strength, she was able to tighten the connection and consequently fix the spray. But my strength was not doing it. I disconnected the hose with no plan in mind and proceeded to reconnect it, hoping by some miracle it would work. Well, it did not. The spray continued from the hose connection. After four attempts to finish watering my vegetables and plants, I gave up and retreated into the house for dry clothes.

I attempted to work on my printer, as it was not producing a clear printout. When I failed at that attempt, I returned to the garden. I looked at the hose and said, "Okay, what's wrong?" I immediately recalled a word from Sunday's message and my morning devotional reading. The word was *alignment*. God was talking about the importance of our alignment with the word of God to gain the prize. He was showing me in the natural.

Now dressed in dry clothes, I looked at both ends of the connection and saw they both had ridges. I carefully lined up the ridges and turned them gently until connected. I turned on the water slowly. With my eyes closed, I heard no spray of water hitting the house and felt no spray of water on my clothes. The connections were properly aligned—success! It was the same with the printer. I reloaded the paper and aligned the paper in the slot, making sure it had a proper fit. Success!

It was a revelation: When we are aligned with God, when we know who He is, and when we know what He can do, prayers get answered, miracles happen, and things work out for good. Listen as He speaks in the natural to reveal the spiritual.

2

BE AWARE

The Lord has many ways to get our attention. He wants a relationship with us and will customize the communication. Will it be a dream, a sermon, a license plate, nature, or a still, small voice? Sometimes a Bible verse will jump off the page into your heart and speak to the trial you are currently going through. It could be a doubt that arises while teaching third- and fourth-graders or a dream that becomes a reality. Follow the desire to want more. Desires are a strong feelings not just a feeling but a *strong* feeling. The Bible tells us that God gives us the desires of our hearts. Take time to connect to God; He is talking all the time. He will tell you great and wonderful things. Most of all, He will tell you He loves you. He will send berries.

3

HOPE IN YOUR TRIAL

I was recently in a situation where a sister in the Lord unknowingly wielded words that were an arrow from the enemy. She had ongoing business with people who had caused me great hurt and loss. She went on to say how successful and fun they were. Despite being the mature Christian I think I am, I received the arrow and allowed it to produce all the pain and misery it was meant to cause. It drove me right into the pit of despair. I was able to grab hold of myself and ask the Lord, *What was that? A trial? A test? A learning opportunity? Lord, what is the strategy when the devil sends us an arrow?* My quiet time with the Lord for the next couple of days produced a plan. It began with me asking myself, *what would Jesus do? What does a Christian reaction look like?*

I took a gift to the person and thanked her for the courtesy she had indeed extended to me in the form of a discount for my purchase. I told her I prayed for her and thanked God that she was in a position to pray for salvation and repentance, especially for those with whom she had an ongoing relationship and any others she may encounter who may benefit from prayer. I told her how special she was to have that opportunity.

Two days later, after a morning quiet time in which I prayed the usual blessings and needs for my family, I heard a tune in my head that would not go away. So I asked the Lord for the words. Most of the day, nothing came to mind. Suddenly, the answer came later that night. It was "Pomp and Circumstance," a military marching song created by Sir Edward Elgar. It was the music played at graduations; it seemed I may have graduated from a course of biblical strategy. Nobody can tell me the Lord has no sense of humor. I grew, and the enemy got a black eye. Mission accomplished.

4

PRACTICE YOUR KNOWING

Scripture tells us that we can hear God's voice.

> My sheep hear my voice, and I know them, and they
> follow me, and I give them Eternal life, and they shall
> never perish, neither shall anyone snatch them Out of
> my hand. (John 10:27–28)

The world calls it intuition; we call it God's voice. Have you ever had a nagging thought that wouldn't leave? You either do something about it or let it nag you all day. The only way you will learn to hear His voice is if you respond to the nagging. So you make the call or send a message to the friend or relative. The response might be, "How did you know?" "Who told you?" or "I needed to hear that today." These and many other responses will let you know God was speaking to you. This is where we learn to rest in Him. Know that He is in control when the nagging thoughts go away, that you just did or experienced God's will for that moment. Those nagging thoughts could be a conviction or a need to forgive or to promote an action. When they no longer dominate your mind, you have done what needed to be done. Goal accomplished. You will have reached the rest in Him that is such a blessing and gift from our Father. You will know that you are walking in the will of God, for you have taken His hand. Practice your knowing, learn to hear one of the ways God speaks to us, and come into His rest.

5

COMFORT AND ENCOURAGEMENT

Have you ever looked around while at a restaurant or an airport and watched the people? Some are deep in thought or, more often in today's world, connected to earbuds or their phones. I would imagine everyone has an issue or concern that could use prayer. What would be my prayer for that person, the one sitting next to me on the plane or across the room? I don't know that person's needs, religion, beliefs, or what to pray for. I would feel embarrassed to go up to someone and say, "Can I pray for you?" In some cases that might be accepted and appropriate.

My thoughts today are this. Take a silent moment to offer a prayer of salvation, comfort, and encouragement for that person sitting in the seat next to you or across the room. The Lord will bless you, for you are doing His will. It is the desire of our Lord to have all people living eternally with Him forever. You may try to rationalize by thinking, *well, they might worship God in other ways or have different doctrines and beliefs.*

Luke 9:50 says, "But Jesus said to him, 'Do not forbid him, for he who is not against us is on our side.'"

Do not underestimate the power of prayer.

6

GETTING TO KNOW YOU

Did you ever think about how you came to believe in God? Were you brought up attending church, Sunday school, or vacation Bible school, or did you say bedtime prayers with your parents? All good stuff. That's where you were able to hear about Him. I believe you didn't get to know Him until you were in a place when all you could do was call out, "Jesus, help me!"

Then a brother or sister from church came alongside you. Friends gave you their testimony about a similar situation they were in and got through. Someone prayed with you and gave you a word of encouragement. A scripture verse in a card spoke volumes of wisdom and encouragement to you and the situation that you were in. My dear friend, you have found the very heart of Jesus and the relationship He wants to have with us. He invades your circumstances; He speaks to your heart. He uses people, scripture, and nature so you will know Him and believe in His word and power. Through your situation, He has gotten your attention. Pick up the Bible and see what else He has for you today. How did those people know to come alongside you? The prompting of the Holy Spirit put you on their hearts so they would reach out to you. They obeyed, not knowing what was going on with you. That's spiritual communication. Don't hang up. Don't log off. Keep the connection.

7

A MOTHER'S LOVE

Just some thoughts today on a mother's love. It comes in so many forms and so many levels of demonstration: outward hugs, quiet encouragement, sometimes nothing but silence, outbursts of anger to a situation, or a look of disapproval to a behavior. It takes time, maybe years, until we can count it all as love.

It is the same with our heavenly parent. Who also wants the very best for our lives? Count all this that we experience as good, for it refines us to be the best that we can be. Our mothers' demonstrations of love are in the natural, and they give us a look and an example of love from the heavens.

8

JOY

How do you start your day? I start with a list that says, "Things to do today." I began to realize that God had a list too. He has a plan as to whom you will meet today. The friend you meet at the library may need a hug or word of encouragement. Smile at the grocery checkout or the customer service person who might be having a bad day. As you are accomplishing your list, be mindful of His list. You will be blessed and become aware of God using you for His purposes and working in you.

Hebrews 13:21 says, "Make you complete in every good work to do His will, working in you what is well pleasing in His sight, through Jesus Christ, to whom be glory forever and ever Amen."

Does your list include things you need or things you want? If you are on a budget, that's a good question to ask yourself. When that charge card bill comes in, the joy of the purchase will disappear. Where do we look for a lasting joy?

Last week as I began to plant some vegetables, I noticed that some perennials I had planted last fall were beginning to show some green spouts. It made me happy, and I felt joy. I take a peek every morning to see the progress of these plants. It may sound silly to you, but not to me. It brought me joy at no cost. Find what lifts your spirit, what no-cost thing brings you joy. My sister often told a story about her friend, who was a new grandmother. Every time she went to visit her grandchild, she always had a shopping bag filled with treats, a new book, or a new toy. One day the grandchild asked for her to bring a specific item the next time she visited. Her friend responded, "Well, maybe your other grandmother could get that for you." The child replied, "She doesn't have a shopping bag." Why that brings laughter and joy to my soul only God knows. Find your no-cost joy; it will last and can be repeated as you recall it. Find your joy in Him.

9

PRAYER

Do you pray? How do you pray? Jesus teaches us and give us the words.

> Our father in heaven, Hallowed be your name. Your kingdom come. Your will be done, on earth as it is in heaven. Give us this day our daily bread and forgive us our debts, as we forgive our debtors. And do not lead us into temptation, but deliver us from the evil one. For yours is the kingdom and power and the glory, forever. Amen. (Matthew 6:9–13)

It's very simple and very clear. His will for us is to prosper and be saved, to walk with Him in the spirit and spend eternity with Him. We pray thy will be done. We forgive because it does more for us than for those who have hurt us. It sets our minds free from rethinking the hurt. Most of all, we are forgiven of our sin by our Father in heaven. It is an important part of prayer.

We can also make our requests known to God through prayer.

I gave testimony to that in my book. One night, I took a wrong exit coming home from a family celebration in an unfamiliar area. It was after midnight as I drove aimlessly to find my way. My prayer was one of fear and desperation. The Lord sent an angel in a large truck with mud flaps that read "Transportation for Christ." The kindly gentleman led me to the road I needed to continue my journey home. He was very present in my time of need. God hears the heartfelt cry of His people.

10

ANGELS ALL AROUND

This week brought some disturbing news about a family that was robbed as they were at work and at school. I was greatly touched in speaking with them about the incident. They shared that it was not the material things that concerned them but that their peace and safety were taken. A police officer interviewed the family. He noted that they were a Christian family who knew and served the Lord. Upon his interview with the twelve year old, he sensed the young man's fears and unsettled emotions. He asked him if he knew Jesus, and the young man replied that, yes, he did. The officer responded, "Well, then, He is your protector and will give you strength." The police officer also shared that he had been doing investigations for a long time. He assured the family that thieves rarely return to a house they have robbed. He was the right person at the right time. Our Lord's time is perfect and always on time. Praise God! Angels come in many forms to remind us of an ever-present God and to put a smile on a young man's face to ease his fears. Jesus used that police officer to bring some comfort to a distressed family. The officer called within a few days to report that the thief had been caught and was in jail. We serve a mighty God.

11

LOOK TO THE HORIZON

I was recently asked to share my thoughts with a group of young women believers. I sat down with the Lord that bright sunny morning outside my back porch beside my newly planted garden and waited on the Lord. I was brought back to a memory of myself when I was their age. How different my thoughts of God were back then. It was only when life began to happen to me that the revelation came and my relationship with God began to evolve through the deaths of close family, parents, and siblings as well as betrayal and the death of a marriage.

> These things I have spoken to you, that in Me you may have peace. In the world you will have tribulation: but be of good cheer; I have overcome the world. (John 16:33)

I can give them my testimony and tell them about my walk, my thoughts, and my prayers. The most important advice I will leave with them is to keep their eyes on the horizon.

Sailors are taught to look to the horizon when they feel seasick to help gain a sense of perspective. If you are overwhelmed, confused, frustrated, or dizzy, you might be seasick. Look to the maker of the horizon.

He drew a circular horizon on the face of the waters, at
the boundary of light and darkness. (Job 26:10)

It is in the times of seasickness that you will receive revelation and relationship with God. You will gain perspective in your situation. It will come layer by layer. I can't give that. I can't speak that to others. That part of revelation is between God and you because it is personal and designed for the plan and purpose God has for you. My encouragement to you and the young ladies I was speaking with is to keep your eyes on the maker of the horizon. I believe you will see the "Son" rise in your life.

12

A MERRY HEART

A merry heart does good, like medicine, but a broken spirit dries the bones. (Proverbs 17:22)

What a gift laughter is, and what a gift to laugh at ourselves. Can we laugh in every situation? I think not. When we can, let's laugh. Laughter releases endorphins and gives us a sense of peace and hope. I want to share a funny childhood story and then look at what God gives us to laugh at.

I was four or five and lived in a second-floor apartment in Brooklyn on Berry Street. The owners of the building were an older couple with no children who lived beneath us. We walked in slippers around the apartment to keep the noise at a minimum as part of our rental agreement. Visitors had to ring a bell to gain entrance into a foyer decorated with glass-framed pictures that included a staircase leading to our apartment. My mother's two brothers, Frank and Mario, always the jokers, rang the bell one night after ten o'clock. My mom pressed the buzzer to let them in, thinking something must be wrong. They would never come over at that hour knowing the rules of our strict landlord. As they ascended the stairs, each of them held a framed picture in his hands. My mother backed up into the apartment with her hands over her mouth to stifle her laughter. After enduring my father's harsh glare at the situation, we collapsed in laughter in a group hug, hands over our mouths. The rest of the visit remained within the landlord's rules with controlled giggles. The pictures were replaced without harm, so there was no repercussion from the landlord. We laughed for years reliving that night. Outside of the apartment, our laughter could be as loud and as long as we wanted as we relived that night and shared the story with others.

And Sarah said, "God has made me laugh, and all who hear will laugh with me." (Genesis 21:6)

> Then the Lord opened the mouth of the donkey and she said to Balaam, "What have I done to you that you have struck me these three times?" (Numbers 22:28)

> Then his brother's wife shall come to him in the presence of the elders, remove his sandal from his foot, spit in the face and answer and say, "So shall it be done to the man who will not build up his brother's house." (Deuteronomy 25:9)

> Then the trees said to the fig tree, "You come and reign over us!" But the fig tree said to them, "Should I cease my sweetness and my good fruit, and go to sway over trees?" (Judges 9:10–11)

> Then our mouth was filled with laughter, and our tongue with singing. Then they said among the nations, "The LORD has done great things for them." (Psalm 126:2)

Sarah laughs, the donkey talks, a shoe is used to discipline a man, and trees talk to one another. Our God has a sense of humor. With respect to the message, I believe our God wants us to laugh.

Have a great day, and may you find laughter along the way— berries, too.

13

OUR GOD HEALS

In my previous book I share how God healed my daughter. I have heard testimony and observed many people and relationships that have been healed on my walk with God. I know our God heals. I recently had to have several extractions and a root canal procedure to correct a dental issue. Not wanting to have any more such issues, I put a request for healthy teeth on my prayer list. My dental problems began as I was traveling to my great-granddaughter's dedication in Maryland. Yes, I am a great-grandmother. *Gigi* is my title. I had a painful toothache with swelling and was able to see the dentist the day after I returned home to resolve the issue. Fast-forward now to baby's first birthday. The trip was scheduled to take place in a few days, but I had a tooth that was beginning to throb and become sensitive to hot and cold. Not wanting to miss this important celebration, I decided to wait until my return from Maryland before making an appointment with the dentist. I prayed and believed that the tooth would not cause the pain and swelling that had occurred on my previous visit. As I was watching *The 700 Club* the day before we were to leave, Terry had a word of knowledge for several people whom God was healing. Just before they finished praying, she said, "There is an issue with a tooth, and God is healing that." It was a wonderful weekend. God cares for the hairs on our heads and the teeth in our mouths. I had no pain and no swelling. I admit that I let my hot morning coffee swirl over that tooth. Praise God—thank you for healing me.

> Bless the Lord, my soul, and forget not all His benefits who forgives all your iniquities, and heals all your disease. (Psalm 103:2–3)

14

THE DOOR

I had new doors installed recently. The old ones had become warped and begun to shift as the warmer weather arrived. They didn't close properly, and one was hard to open. It made me think about a painting by William Holman Hunt of Jesus knocking on a door while holding a lantern. *What's a door?* I thought. *A protector, a separation, provides entrance, welcomes.*

> "Most assuredly, I say to you, he who does not enter by the sheepfold by the door but climbs up some other way, he is a thief and a robber. But he who enters by the door is a shepherd of the sheep. To him the doorkeeper opens, and the sheep hear his voice, and he calls his own sheep by name, and leads them out."… Jesus therefore said to them again, "Most assuredly, I say to you, I am the door of the sheep." (John 10:1–3, 7)

In the painting, the door has no outside handle. It must be opened from the inside by us. This is something to ponder today on our journey to relationship with the Father. As we stand inside the door, let us recall all the blessings, gifts, and promises that await on the other side of the door. It's a good thing to keep your door well maintained so it can open easily.

15

THE REWARD OF QUIET TIME

When we make the effort to set aside time to be quiet with the Lord, there is reward. Some of us have to fight for that time because of worldly concerns and fears. Do fight for this special time. Reject all thoughts that do not align with God's character. Recall and reflect on the words in the scriptures.

Accept the invitation.

> Then the Lord said to Noah, "Come into the ark, you and all your household, because I have seen that you are righteous before me in this generation." (Genesis 7:1)

> "And as for me, behold, I establish My covenant with you and with your descendants after you." (Genesis 9:9)

Completely impossible situation not even going to pray about it. Sarah thought so too.

> And Sarah said, "God has made me laugh, and all who hear will laugh with me." (Genesis 21:6)

Yes Sarah we are laughing too. Welcome, Isaac, the promise. God is always faithful.

Big problem, overwhelming, huge situation.

> And the Philistine said to David, "Come to me, and I will give your flesh to the birds of the air and the beasts of the field!" Then David said to the Philistine, "You come to me with a sword with a spear, and with a javelin, but I come to you in the name of the LORD of hosts, the God of the armies of Israel, whom you have defied." (1 Samuel 17:44–45)

When God is in the battle, He wins. Be encouraged.

Hopefully we will emerge from our quiet time encouraged by God's word.

16

GIFTS FROM ABOVE

We can hear that gentle whisper in our quiet time but also as we are loading the dishwasher. Keep your ears attentive as you contemplate your worries and concerns throughout the day, focusing on Jesus.

We had an awesome church service this Sunday. Every gift of the Holy Spirit was present. A word of knowledge was delivered in tongues with an interpretation of tongues. Testimonies of healing and deliverance came forth. Wisdom from the word was read aloud. The love and peace of the Spirit came over the congregation as we worshiped in song. All these things produced increased faith in God and who He is, the great I AM. These incredible gifts are blessings that must not go unnoticed, so take a moment today to ask and pray for an increase in spiritual gifts. They are ours for the asking

> But the manifestation of the Spirit is given to each one for the profit of all: for to one is given the word of wisdom through the Spirit, to another a word of knowledge through the same Spirit. To another faith by the same spirit, to another gifts of healings by the same Spirit, to another the working of miracles, to another prophecy, to another discerning of spirits, to another different

kinds of tongues, to another the interpretation of tongues. (1 Corinthians 12:7–10)

Fellowship followed the service, and evident in the atmosphere were clearly the fruits of the spirit.

The fruits of the Spirit are love, joy, peace, patience, kindness, goodness, faithfulness, gentleness, self-control; against such things there is no law. (Galatians 5:22–23)

Let us not take for granted the spiritual gifts available to us every day. We must grow in what our Father has available for us. He wants to give us good things. Listen for the whisper. May your day be filled with spiritual blessings.

17

SEVEN TIMES SEVENTY

I don't think there are many of us who have not experienced hurt, disappointment, injustice, or betrayal. Jesus tells us in the scriptures how to handle these situations.

> Then Peter came to Him and said, "Lord, how often shall my brother sin against me, and I forgive him? Up to seven times?" Jesus said to him, "I do not say to you, up to seven times, but up to seventy times seven." (Matthew 18:21–22)

Our flesh and the world have very different approaches. Be honest—most of us would like to use the worldly solution rather than the biblical solution. I have learned through His grace and trials that forgiveness is a process and comes in layers. When the shock of an incident lessens to some extent and you can reconnect with the word of God, you can start the process. This takes place between you and God. If the offender is not in the picture, that's all right. It is God that needs to know your heart. Forgiveness does not necessarily mean having a relationship with the offender. This act of obeying the word puts us where we need to be to heal and recover. It also frees the mind from replaying the offense.

The hard part comes when a situation, song, person, stranger, or something else triggers a response in you that brings the pain of the offense back as fresh as the day it happened. Not seven times but up to seventy times seven times you say to yourself that you forgive again. Jesus had that right, like He knew. Of course He knew.

The harder part is that, as life goes on, more triggers surface. Seventy times seven, seventy times seven—the process continues to heal and restore. Be encouraged today that your obedience is not in vain.

> For if you forgive men their trespasses, your heavenly
> Father will also forgive you. (Matthew 6:14)

May God in His infinite mercy bless you as you process His forgiveness.

18

GOING THROUGH SOMETHING?

Why are you cast down, O my soul? And why are you disquieted within me? Hope in God, for I shall yet praise Him for the help of His countenance. (Psalm 42:1)

The word that jumped out at me was *again*. Oh, how soon we forget the last time He came through for us and what He has done so far. Let us focus on those things and be confident that He will do it again. Take your finger off the replay button that brings despair and disturbance to your soul. Focus on your surroundings.

Is there a bird singing outside your window? Did your church sister, neighbor, or friend call to pray with you and to ask how you are doing today? Oh, and the lady at the checkout counter—did she smile at you and tell you to have a great day? Did you get a nod from a driver who let you exit into the flow of traffic? Did you get that parking spot close to the store's entrance? These are not coincidences; they are God incidents. When the replay button in our minds is pressed, we can miss these simple ways God speaks.

I call these incidents berries. These small, sweet things that are good for our health are ours for the picking and taste so good, especially when in season. They add to our spiritual health when we choose to pick them and recognize them as being from God. They are sweetness to our souls, especially when they come in the season of despair When we are walking in the forest and can't see the tress, we need only look for the berries. They are all around us. Be encouraged today. He will never leave you nor forsake you and will work everything for good to those who love him.

19

WAITING FOR THE PROMISE

Is it a vision, a promise that has not yet come to pass?

> Saying, "Surely blessing I will bless you, and multiplying
> I will multiply you." And so after he had patiently
> endured, he obtained the promise. (Hebrews 6:14–15)

The wait has a purpose, always. He is growing your patience. He is expanding your faith. He is developing your trust in Him. He is giving you the time to forgive the offense against you, past or present. It's time for alignment in the spirit. It's the road to a higher education and a degree in godly ways. The wait has a purpose.

Don't give up in the dry times. Continue to pray and seek His wisdom and direction to stay on track. Trust His timing, and be sure to hear clearly from Him in regard to the promise or vision. It is not a good idea to listen to others. Abram listened to the voice of Sarai and got into a ton of trouble.

> So Sarai said to Abram, "See now, the Lord has
> restrained me from bearing children. Please,
> go in to my maid: perhaps I shall obtain
> children by her." And Abram heeded the
> voice of Sarai. (Genesis 16:2)

So proceed with caution. If it's God's plan it will be carried out in His timing and His way, without you doing a thing to accomplish it.

Be of good courage, and He shall strengthen your heart.
All you who hope in the Lord. (Psalm 31:24)

20

SAMSON AND DELILAH

I spent some time in the Catskill Mountains recently. As I viewed the beauty of the surrounding area, I recalled a conversation I had as a child with my father. My family spent many summers in this area when I was growing up. My memories include happy, carefree days of swimming in the creeks and hiking the many trails. What stands out the most is my father's smile as he recalled the mountain range of the area in Italy where he spent the first seventeen years of his life. His joy was evident. As we viewed this picturesque mountain range that filled the horizon, my father traced its shape with his finger. The shape of the mountain range was similar in appearance to a giant bear lying down sleeping. Most evenings near sunset we would watch as this scene faded into the night. As I recalled this sweet memory, another giant came to mind. This giant also fell asleep and lost his strength, but God supplied the need and he was victorious in the end. This giant was Samson

> Then she lulled him to sleep on her knees, and called
> for a man and had him shave off the seven locks of his
> head. Then she began to torment him and his
> strength left him. (Judges 16:19)

I know we all think at times we are giants and we can do it all. The truth is that we fall asleep in our trials and lose strength.

> Then Samson called to the Lord, saying, "O Lord, remember me, I pray! Strengthen me, I pray, just this once, O God that I may with one blow take vengeance on the Philistines for my two eyes!" (Judges 16:28)

God answered that prayer, and Samson had the victory. He will do the same for us.

> I can do all things through Christ who strengthens me. (Philippians 4:13)

21

THE GIFT OF CRITICAL THINKING

A guest speaker at a college graduation ceremony I attended recently talked about the important aspects of a higher education. He applauded the students' academic accomplishments and the achievement of their goals. He went on to speak of one more course they hadn't signed up for but had no doubt taken. That was the course in the art of critical thinking. This skill, he continued, would be the one most likely help them in their career decisions, personal relationships, and so much more as they left this institution of higher learning. He said it would be a guide to success and offer peace of mind that they had made the right decisions. My thoughts went to how this might apply to our spiritual lives.

> Finally, brethren, whatever things are true, whatever things are noble, whatever things are just, whatever things are pure, whatever things are lovely, and whatever things are of good report, if there is any virtue and if there is anything praiseworthy meditate on these things. (Philippians 4:8–9)

God, our institute of higher learning, is saying that we should critique our thoughts to weed out the nasty, negative, and hurtful things and find peace. We need to do this to find success in our day-to-day lives. To grow in critical thinking is to walk in the spirit.

> For to be carnally minded is death, but to be spiritually minded is life and peace. (Romans 8:6)

Shall we sign up for the course? Grab your Bibles. School is starting this week.

22

HOW ARE YOUR BERRIES?

Remember earlier that I talked about berries? They are sweet little things that taste good, are packed with nutrients, and are so good for our health. That's all good stuff, in the natural. God has what I call berries in the spirit too. Berries are usually found in the forest along a path or trail. When you are on that path in a dark place and have lost your way, look for berries.

God wants us to know that there are berries in the spirit and look for them. They are all around us, as He promises never to leave us or forsake us. One of my berries came on a dark, cold November night when I made a wrong turn and was so lost. It was midnight, and a white tractor trailer cab pulled up beside me. I asked the driver for directions, and he helped me to get to a familiar road that led me home. "Transportation for Christ" was printed on his mud flaps and shone brightly in the overhead lights as he pulled away and left me to continue my journey. That was a sweet berry that propelled my faith to new heights. Don't stop looking for berries. God is concerned about our spiritual health.

I recently had to have surgery in an area near my neck, and it resulted in damage to my vocal cords. "Not unusual," the doctor stated. "Should return within a month." Five months later I still couldn't speak above a whisper and sometimes not at all. *All right, Lord,* I thought, *I will take this time to listen and pray that all will be well. Maybe He is expanding my trust by letting me travel on a road that was at times dark and confusing.* One day after leaving an intercessors' prayer meeting, I pulled into traffic. As I slowed down at a red light, a panel truck pulled alongside, and written on the side of the truck in bold letters was "Total Restoration Services." My voice returned a week later, and my faith and trust went up another notch. I never saw that truck again.

How is your berry patch? Has God showed up in a special, unusual, or personal way to give you a sweet, nutritional lift to your spiritual walk? I would love to hear about it and for you to share. Jesus said in Luke 21:13, "But it will turn out for you as an occasion for testimony."

DISCOVER YOUR GIFTS

Exodus tells us that God gave manna and quail to the sons of Israel. He supplied a navigation device in the form of a cloud.

> Then I will give them one heart, and I will put a new spirit within them, and take the stony heart out of their flesh, and give them a heart of flesh. (Ezekiel 11:19)

Our God is constantly giving gifts to us freely. This is not a surprise; He loves us. It is up to us to discover the gifts and use them for His glory.

> But the manifestation of the Spirit is given to each one for the profit of all. (1 Corinthians 12:7)

> But Peter said to him, "Your money perish with you, because you thought that the gift of God could be purchased with money! (Acts 8:20)

Heads up—we can't buy gifts from God. They are freely given by our Father. We know what they are. They are those things that come easily to us, what we are passionate about. They are our gifts given to us from our Father to be used for and in the kingdom of God. Do you teach or maybe host? Can you organize easily? Can you write, speak, sew, knit, or bake? Can you play a musical instrument or maybe sing? So many more things are given to us.

Some have a few gifts. Some have one. But we all have received. Dig deep, discover it, and recognize it for what it is. It's His gift to you, personally. Use it for His glory in His name, for Him who gives freely.

> For the gifts and the calling of God are irrevocable.
> (Romans 11:29)

24

HEALINGS AND THOUGHTS

My thoughts today are on how God heals and restores, even from death.

> And he said to her "Give me your son." Then he took the child from her arms and carried him up to the upper room where he was staying and laid him on his own bed. (1 Kings 17:19)

God restores the child to good health, but my heart wonders if the response to "give me your son" was the key to this healing. It is when we surrender all that God honors our request.

> Then Isaiah said, "Take a lump of figs." So they took it and laid it on the boil, and he recovered. (2 Kings 20:7)

> When He had said these things, He spat on the ground and made clay with the saliva, and He anointed the eyes of the blind man with the clay. (John 9:6)

Can we obey even if what God says sounds weird and hard to do? Forgive and pray for those who hurt you. Victory is in obedience.

Which is easier, to say to the paralytic, "Your sins are forgiven," or to say, "Arise and take up your bed and walk?" Immediately he rose, took up the bed, and went out in the presence of them all, so that all were amazed and glorified God, saying, "We never saw anything like this!" (Mark 2:9–12)

I feel that this might mean that we should stop the pity party, stand on God's word and our spiritual feet, and walk with Him.

Then Peter said, "Silver and gold I do not have, but what I do have I give you. In the name of Jesus Christ of Nazareth, rise up and walk." And He took him by the right hand and lifted him up, and immediately his feet and ankle bones received strength. (Acts 3:6–7)

This makes me think, are we asking and praying for the right things from our all-powerful, giving God? Is obedience what He is teaching us? We need to listen to that still, small voice, that sensing of the Holy Spirit deep within our hearts; to hear His voice in a message spoken; and to believe.

25

SOMEBODY IS STEALING
YOUR VINEYARD

Concerning our generational blessings, we all know the story of Joseph and his life in Egypt. Jacob was near death when he gathered Joseph and Joseph's sons, Ephraim and Manasseh, to transfer the blessings he had received from God to the next generation. He lay his hands on his sons and also prophesied over them that they were to become the twelve tribes of Israel. In speaking to Joseph, he proclaimed him as a fruitful bough by a fruitful spring. Jacob passed to his sons the blessing he received from God.

> Behold I will make you fruitful and multiply you, and I
> will make of you a multitude of people, and I will give
> this land to your descendants after you as an everlasting
> possession. (Genesis 48:4)

Five generations later, we met Naboth, the Jezreelite. He had a beautiful, lush vineyard next to the palace where Ahab resided as the king of Samaria. Naboth was enjoying his spiritual inheritance. Every day Ahab looked over at the lush vineyard and finally decided he would like to have that lush land to make a vegetable garden for himself. He went over to Naboth's home, offered a fair price for the land, and was surprised at Naboth's response:

> But Naboth said to Ahab, "The Lord forbid me that I should give the inheritance of my fathers to you." (1 Kings 21:3)

> The land shall not be sold permanently, for the land is mine: for you are strangers and sojourners with me. (Leviticus 25:23)

This put Ahab into a deep depression. He resorted to taking some ungodly advice from his wife, Jezebel, and had Naboth killed. He could now take over the land for his vegetable garden for his own use. Oh, dear.

This part of scripture tells us about the land, generational blessings, and inheritance—all so very important to our walk. When we receive these blessings, we walk in the glory and grace provided by them, but we may become the target of envy. What's stealing your vineyard, your inheritance, and your blessings? Who is stealing your peace and joy? The inheritance is meant for a specific purpose; vineyard to vegetable garden does not agree with God's purpose. Guard your vineyard for God's purpose. Guard your legacy, your gifts, and your ministry. God bless you and keep you.

26

BE STILL AND KNOW THAT I AM GOD

Is the enemy chasing you today? Coming in like a flood? Trying to do his best work? Give him no place or authority over you or your situation. Stand still. There is power in being still. The enemy will be confused as to why you have no reaction to his plan. That's fun to think about.

> Listen to this, O Job. Stand still and consider the wondrous works of God. (Job 37:14)

Job did stand still, and at the end of the book of Job, the reward he was given is evident. Job was strong; maybe we are not as strong. We may have to ask our Father in heaven for help and for strength before we can stand still. Standing still is an effective weapon in a spiritual battle. Reading the word and beholding his wondrous works is standing still.

> Be still, and know that I am God: I will be exalted among the nations I will be exalted in the earth! The Lord of hosts is with us: the God of Jacob is our refuge. Selah (Psalm 46:10)

Standing still is still standing.

27

IMAGES OF A WORSHIP SERVICE

I was recently invited to visit a church service by friends who experienced a sudden deliverance from lifelong abuse of alcohol and drugs. I felt led to go and worship there one Sunday morning with this newfound community. I was greeted warmly by a group of about forty-five people representing many age groups.

Through my years of being a Christian, I have attended numerous worship services. While they were all wonderful times of worship and time spent in the presence of the Lord, several stand out as memorable, one being in the Ukraine. After landing in Kiev, we went to a church that hosted incoming and outgoing teams who came to minister in their country. Together with the outgoing team, we worshiped—they in gratitude of what God had accomplished, and we in anticipation of what God was about to do. The outgoing teams, though weary and fatigued, worshiped with the awesome knowledge of the power of God on the mission field. We, fresh and eager to serve, became strengthened and prepared to go forward and serve. It was a worship service of God's power.

Another service of worship that I was blessed to be a part of was in South Africa. I still listen to a recording of the service, and it continues to bring me to the level of worship I witnessed while in a little village there. The people's newfound belief in God generates an unshakable faith as God works in their hearts and minds. It produces a belief that reflects in their worship and a hunger for the word that results in a worship service to behold. It was a worship service of hope and belief.

One service that I was invited to on a beautiful fall morning added to my memorable worship services list. Many of the congregants, including the pastor, had previously seen the deliverance and salvation of some of the worst addictions and medical and family situations the enemy can come up with. Some old and some young have seen the impossible become possible, all through the mighty, miraculous hand of God. Some older people had received deliverance later in life, while younger ones had received the deliverance quickly. It is my belief that God has a plan for this younger generation and is doing a quick work for a time such as this. The power and presence of God was so heavy that day in the small group of believers. They had seen His hand in their lives and realized it could only be God who accomplished this new life they had. The worship was sweet yet powerful enough to bring the presence of God into the service. They knew that they knew, for they saw. It was the highest form of worship we can give Him. There was no struggle. It was a worship service of rest in Him.

> Come to me, all you who labor and are heavy-laden,
> and I will give you rest. (Matthew 11:28)

> I have heard of you by the hearing of the ear. But now
> my eye sees you. (Job 42:5)

Berries all around.

HOPE DEFERRED

Hope deferred makes the heart sick, but when the desire comes, it is the tree of life. (Proverbs 13:12)

The tree of life symbolizes the achievement of a deeply felt desire. It is like coming back to the Garden of Eden. How do we avoid becoming heartsick? First, as we talked about before, look for the helpers. A word or phrase that speaks to you through a scripture you are reading or a song that stops your thoughts and speaks to your circumstance. God is present and speaking all the time. Have you gotten any berries today? You know, the sweet little things that infuse your spirit with joy. Maybe it was an extra discount at the checkout; a parking spot in front of the store you needed to go into when your feet were aching; a phone call, smile, or kind words; or a "God bless you" from a stranger. These are the favor of the Lord—berries. Hang in there for whatever the Lord has put on your heart to hope for. Your deep desire comes from His heart. It is His desire. Walk with Him every day and listen to the encouragement and love He gives.

I recently had to have some renovations done in my home. I never left my home during the process and had more helpers and berries than I could count. Right now I have Robert here, cleaning my vents. He told me about how he and his sister have found sobriety and an awareness of God and faith. God led him to a life free of alcohol. I shared my book to encourage his journey. Any deferred hope that I may have been feeling was dispelled today. The nineteen-year-old electrician's helper who was delivered in a crack house is now being mentored by a pastor and his wife. There's also the carpet salesman who leads a marriage ministry with his wife. The young painter I hired from the maintenance crew to paint my living room who needed to hear the good news and for whom God opened the door for me to give it. The electrician who was delivered of drugs and alcohol in a prison cell after over thirty years of abuse and is now sober and using the gifts given to him. These are some of the helpers and berries I received, and I never left the house. Friends and family who helped me through a recent health issue are also berries. Imagine how much more is out in our neighborhoods as we walk with Him and become aware of His presence and what He is doing.

> But those who wait upon the Lord shall renew their strength, they shall mount up with wings like eagles. They shall run, and not be weary. They shall walk, and not faint. (Isaiah 40:31)

29

HOW IS YOUR WITNESS?

It has been a busy Thanksgiving weekend. Most of us, I am sure, are spending it with relatives we have not seen for a while or don't see too often. Some of them believe in God, some don't, and some believe in their own way. So what does the Bible say, as it is our instruction manual for these situations? God gives us the blueprint.

> Beloved, I beg you as sojourners and pilgrims, abstain from fleshly lusts which war against the soul. Having your conduct honorable among the Gentiles, that when they speak against you as evildoers, they may by your good works which they observe, glorify God in the day of visitation. Therefore submit yourselves to every ordinance of man for the Lord's sake, whether to the king as supreme, or to governors, as to those who are sent by him for the punishment of evildoers and for the praise of those who do good. For this is the will of God, that by doing good you may put to silence the ignorance of foolish men, as free, yet not using liberty as a cloak for vice, but as bondservants of God. Honor all people, Love the brotherhood. Fear God. Honor the King. (1 Peter 2:11–17)

I pray all went well as you spent time with family and friends. It may be a good idea to keep this scripture in mind as the holidays are quickly approaching. Our lives speak louder than our words. I have always believed that children pick up and learn more from the nonverbal than the verbal.

30

HOW LOVE IS RECEIVED

I did not grow up in a very demonstrative family, but I always felt loved and cherished. Most of my recollections are from my early childhood, as my parents passed at an early age. I recall a smile and a nod of the head, a strong hand patting my back, and a head rub. I remember being called by a pet name and, of course, moments of sharing food. Most of all, I was given boundaries as to the right and wrongs of life. All this I received as a demonstration of their love and recognition of my accomplishments. My most memorable food related moments are from the elementary school gym where we were taken for lunchtime. Some days, my mom would come in with my favorite hot lunch and spend that time just chatting about the day. Somewhere deep in our hearts lies that inner child who longs for that kind of love in our present day. It is available if we are able to recognize and receive the love of Jesus.

It is worthwhile to take a moment, maybe a little more, to explore how God loves just as a parent loves. We share spiritual food, His word, and chat with Him. He gave us life. He forgives. He extends grace and protects. He gives boundaries to life's journey. He provides. He feeds us spiritual food. He saves. All this occurs in the spirit as well as in the natural. He speaks in a still, small voice to direct and give the peace of childhood love, to heal our wounds, and to attend to our concerns. He does it quietly. Let us not miss it or overlook it. We all receive and recognize love differently. This Christmas season, let us celebrate the quiet love of Jesus. How will you receive and recognize His love?

There is a scripture that tells it all. I love it.

> For thus says the Lord of hosts, "He sent me after glory, to the nations which plunder you. For He who touches you, touches the apple of His eye." (Zechariah 2:8)

Now that's a mama bear at her best.

31

GOD IS LIGHT AND LOVE

I am just about finished with a devotional titled *Jesus Calling*. It offered a reminder every day about how involved Jesus wants to be in our day-to-day lives. I began to practice having Him involved in everything that was going on in my day.

Recently I was at a Christmas luncheon for about two hundred women. It was midweek, so I was not surprised that the staff was shorthanded. My assigned table was missing chairs and utensils, and we didn't get coffee cups or a milk-and-sugar setup until we could get the attention of a harried waitress. The plan was for those at the bar area, in front of which I was sitting, to distribute the desserts, apple crisps topped with either vanilla or chocolate ice cream. The problem was that only one young lady was assigned to the task, and the ice cream was frozen solid and very difficult to scoop. The line was endless and the comments relentless and in some instances rude. Midway through the service, another server came to assist. A loud conversation between the two servers ensued, and it sounded like the performance of the helper was not quite up to the standard of the original server. The argument between them caused the latter server to run off in tears, leaving the original server to complete the task with the anxious crowd waiting for dessert. As the line finally came to an end, I felt the Holy Spirit urge me to speak to this lone server during what I am sure was a difficult time. *All right, Lord,* I thought, *you tell me what to say.* Soon I was standing at a bar filled with wine and liquors pouring out His love. I complimented the server on her performance under very difficult circumstances and how well she had handled the rude remarks and advice for improvement during the distribution of the dessert. In tears, she received my words and shared that the young lady who had come to help was her younger sister, who was I am guessing about sixteen. She also shared that things were going on at home that should not have been brought to the workplace.

God is involved in our daily lives for His purpose. He showed up at a women's Christmas luncheon to show love to someone who may not know Him yet but will remember when He loved her. We don't know where people are on their journeys to find Christ or the plan or purpose He has for them. Just be sure to be in the day to day with He who wants to be in your day to day.

> Let your light shine before men, that they may see your good works, and glorify your Father in heaven. (Matthew 5:16)

32

EMMANUEL GOD WITH YOU

Therefore the Lord Himself will give you a sign. Behold, the virgin shall conceive and bear a Son, and shall call His name Immanuel. (Isaiah 7:14)

> And having come in, the angel said to her, "Rejoice, highly favored one, the Lord is with you, blessed are you among women!" But when she saw him, she was troubled at his saying, and considered what manner of greeting this was. Then the angel said to her, "Do not be afraid, Mary, for you have found favor with God. And behold you will conceive in your womb and bring forth a Son, and shall call His name Jesus." (Luke 1:28–31)

A young Jewish girl lived in a small village where, I am sure, everyone knew everyone. Finances and resources limited, she was engaged to a young man named Joseph. She had much to ponder.

> Then Joseph her husband, being a just man and not wanting to make her a public example, was minded to put her away secretly. But while he thought about these things behold an angel of the Lord appeared to him in a

dream, saying, "Joseph, son of David, do not be afraid to take to you Mary as your wife, for the child who has been conceived in her is of the Holy Spirit." (Matthew 1:19–20)

Mary and Joseph pondered and considered their situation. This is an additional gift and teaching to us this season. Lord, teach us to ponder and consider your ways that we find what Mary found as we navigate our mountains and valleys.

And Mary said: "My soul magnifies the Lord, and my spirit has rejoiced in God my Savior. For He has regarded the lowly state of His maidservant. For behold, henceforth all generations will call me blessed. For He who is mighty has done great things for me, and holy is His name. (Luke 1:46–49)

33

PERSEVERANCE

As we are approaching the beginning of a new year, I sat before the Lord asking for direction and some godly wisdom for a time such as this. The first impression I got was hope. This parable came to mind.

> Now there was a widow in that city, and she came to him saying, "Get justice for me from my adversary." And he would not for a while, but afterward he said within himself, "Though I do not fear God nor regard man, yet because this widow troubles me I will avenge her, lest by her continual coming she weary me." Then the Lord said, "Hear what the unjust judge said. And shall God not avenge His own elect who cry out day and night to Him, though He bears long with them? I tell you that He will avenge them speedily. Nevertheless, when the Son of man comes, will He really find faith on earth?" (Luke 18:3–8)

As I continued to seek the Lord, I was brought to the book of Nehemiah. The Lord put on Nehemiah's heart to rebuild the wall around Jerusalem, but he encountered opposition from those who did not agree with this plan.

So it was, from that time on that half of my servants worked on construction, while the other half held the spears, the shields, the bows, and wore armor; and the leaders were behind all the house of Judah. Those who built on the wall and those who carried burdens, loaded themselves so that with one hand they worked at construction, and with the other had held a weapon. Every one of the builders had his sword girded at his side as he built. And the one who sounded the trumpet was beside me. (Nehemiah 4:16–18)

So the wall was finished on the twenty fifth day of Elul, in fifty-two days. And it happened, when all our enemies heard of it, and all the nations around us saw these things, that they were very disheartened in their own eyes; for they perceived that this work was done by our God. (Nehemiah 6:15–16)

Persistence pays off. Weapons were ready. Continue in what God has put on your heart, and equip yourself with the weapons of warfare. Fellowship is important in time of crisis. Victory is ours through God.

I recently received a copy of the *Farmer's Almanac*. As I was looking through its predictions and remedies, I thought about how blessed we are to have the Bible to teach and guide us in the matters of life and this journey that we are all on. It is our legacy, God to us. It is a legacy of hope.

34

THIS YEAR

I was sitting quietly before the Lord yesterday and asked Him what's new for the coming year. I was led to read Paul's letters to the churches. Paul encouraged, taught, and expressed his support and love. Sometimes he corrected and redirected their efforts on their journey to know Christ. Are we called also in a time such as this to disciple those in our sphere of influence? What tools do we have to take on a task such as this?

> It is also written in your law that the testimony of two men is true. (John 8:17)
>
> And they said, "What further testimony do we need? For we have heard it ourselves from His own mouth." (Luke 22:71)

Testimony—we all have one. It is personal to us and powerful because we saw it with our own eyes. It allows us to teach, encourage, support, and love, as well as to disciple. To disciple is to be available, be a friend, teach from past events in your life, to share, and most of all to love.

Finally brethren, pray for us that the word of the Lord may spread rapidly and be gloried, just as it did also with you. (2 Thessalonians 3:1)

Where is my sphere? Where is your sphere? What's a sphere?

A field or area where an individual or organization has power to affect development and events.

Wow, that's our workplaces, our families, our neighborhoods, and our churches. We have lots of spheres. Most of all, we have testimony. Have fun in your sphere.

35

CHANGE OF PLANS

I have been reading Jeremiah 18. Most are familiar with and have heard sermons referring to the potter's wheel.

> The word which came to Jeremiah from the Lord, saying, "Arise and go to the potter's house, and there I will cause you to hear my words." (Jeremiah 18:1–2)

> But now, O Lord you are our Father, We are the clay, and you our potter, and all we are the work of your hand. (Isaiah 64:8)

> And the vessel that he made of clay was marred in the hand of the potter; so he made it again into another vessel, as it seemed good to the potter to make. (Jeremiah 18:4)

God can change plans. That verse in Jeremiah spoke volumes of revelation to me. He can redirect according to His plan. He can remold us. The good thing is we are still in His plan when change comes into our lives. The purpose of the plan is in His hands. Our job is to accept the change as the clay is remolded on the potter's wheel. Find your potter's house, go to it, and the Lord will cause you to hear His words. Find the potter's house where the distractions are few. Maybe it is at the beach, in the car, or at the park. Find it and listen. Are you up for a makeover, a reboot, a remake? It's all good because we are in the hands of the potter, our God, our Father.

36

FAVOR GRACE AND MERCY

I have been reading in the book of Daniel and was impressed by the amount of favor, grace, and mercy that was given to him. After Daniel was released from the lion's den unharmed, the king Darius declares in Daniel 6:25–27:

> To all the peoples, nations, and languages that dwell in all the earth: Peace be multiplied to you. I make a decree that in every dominion of my kingdom men must tremble and fear before the God of Daniel. For He is the living God, and steadfast forever, His kingdom is the one which shall not be destroyed. And His dominion shall endure to the end. He delivers and rescues, And He works signs and wonders in heaven and on earth,. Who has delivered Daniel from the power of the lion.

These blessings came from an unbeliever, a worshiper of false gods and idols. I also thought about Joseph. The same blessings were bestowed on him many generations ago by men who were also unbelievers. Some were believers, like his brothers who wanted him dead for personal gain, but were without revelations or relationship with God. They eventually honored him as did Pharaoh.

Then Pharaoh said to Joseph, "In as much as God has shown you all this, there is no one as discerning and wise as you. You shall be over my house, and all my people shall be ruled according to your word, only in regard to the throne will I be greater than you. (Genesis 41:39–40)

A random thought occurred to me as I pondered these scriptures: What a wise and skillful God we serve. To me it was a hidden gem, a berry, that little sweet thing that boosts my faith. God was blessing His children, always watching out for them, yet He was after the hearts of the unbelievers and creating a testimony for multitudes of people. Praise God!

He has shown you, O man, what is good: And what does the Lord require of you But to do justly, To love mercy, And to walk humbly with your God? (Micah 6:8)

Sweet, like a berry.

37

SOME BITS OF WISDOM FROM ABOVE

Over the many years I have been walking with the Lord and learning to take His hand and walk with Him, He has given me some wisdom that I would like to share with you today.

In the times that I had a decision to make or needed to ask for a solution to a current situation, these little sayings or groups of words would come to mind to address either my situation or the person I was praying for. I began to line them up with the word of God and felt the peace to go ahead and apply them to the situation.

I am just going to list some of phrases and let you determine if they can apply to what you are facing right now.

- It is not what you say but who you are that ministers to others.
- What matters most is not what we leave behind in material things but that which is woven in the lives of our loved ones. (Pericles)
- When you are tired, your emotional response will be off. Rest in Him.
- Stay close to those who have testimony; water their lives. Their experience has the power of God, and they are being led by that power.

- You cannot be filled until you are emptied. (Jacque Watkins)
- There is richness in simplicity.
- Forgiveness does not establish relationship. Relationship is based on trust and is not possible without true change of mind and behavior. We must forgive immediately, and God will complete the healing and restoration. The human spirit cannot accomplish this on their own. (William P. Young)
- A state of completeness is attained when one becomes whole and is able to make decisions without past hurts taking a part in the decision.
- Actions and decisions should be based on human decency and whether you are hurting someone or something.
- Successful relationships are based on the maturity of both parties.
- What is lacking in each of us that needs constant approval and reassurance from others to affirm or build our self-worth?

I hope this has given all of us a little food for thought. There is more, but that's for another time.

38

MORE BITS OF WISDOM

Here are some more bits of wisdom that the Lord has put on my mind and heart to share. I hope some of it speaks to you in your situation.

- When the whirlwind passes, the righteous will stand on a firm foundation. (Proverbs 10:25)
- We have a profound impact on the next generation, no matter what age we are.
- We must live life going forward, but it is understood backward.
- There is growth in darkness.
- Rebirth occurs in the desert.
- The only soul that stays calm in a storm is the one who has been through the storm.
- You have to be willing to let go of the life you planned in order to make room for the life you are meant to live. (Joseph Campbell)
- God will say no if it defies His purpose.
- Be angry, but do not sin.
- When you can't see His hand, trust His heart.

- Don't react, respond.
- The greatest offense we can commit in an intimate relationship is dishonesty.

I pray you have enough to think about and apply to whatever is going on with you today. Stay in God's word. Present your cares and concerns to Him that cares for you. Find your berries.

39

FLIP THE SWITCH

I recently returned from a trip to visit with family and friends that involved four flights—four times waiting to check in, four times waiting to go through security, four times waiting to board, plus all the other waits connected to traveling. We encountered many people while going through the waits.

As I was patiently waiting, I felt the Lord urge me to pray for the people who checked my baggage, who looked at my boarding pass, and who sat in my area while waiting to board. I prayed for salvation and knowledge and most of all relationship with our King and Savior. I felt the Lord was at work to add to His kingdom. These scriptures came to mind as I was praying.

> For it is God who commanded light to shine out of darkness, who has shone in our hearts to give the light of the knowledge of the glory of God in the face of Jesus Christ. (2 Corinthians 4:6)

> … [you] may be able to comprehend with all the saints what is the breadth and length and height and depth, to know the love of Christ which surpassed knowledge,

that you may be filled up to all the fullness of God. (Ephesians 3:18–19)

Every good gift and every perfect gift is from above, and comes down from the Father of lights, with whom there is no variation or shadow of turning. (James 1:17)

I felt I was being used to pray in my sphere of influence at that time, in that place, at that moment. Our prayers turn on the switch that gives the Light; the source is God. All we need to do to help Him is to obey the prompt, and the light will shine. Will we see it? Maybe, but for sure we donated a kilowatt to the light bulb.

WHAT ROAD SHALL I TAKE?

When you wake up and think about the day ahead of you, what are your thoughts? *What should I do first? What should I wear? What's the weather doing? What's for breakfast? Who needs what done for them today?* Sometimes these thoughts are overwhelming when the list goes on and on.

I had one of those days recently, and by 4:15 in the afternoon, nothing had been accomplished. I ran from one chore to the next without accomplishment. The line was so long in returns that I had to leave to be on time for a dentist appointment. The dentist was one hour behind due to an emergency. I tried the return line again and realized I didn't have the right receipt.

The grocery store ran out of the item I was hoping to stock up on. The customer service desk was lined with irate shoppers looking for a rain check. I did wait, because the sale was too good to be true, but I returned home without the item I had hoped to get. I rated the day as a disaster and proceeded home, hoping for the peace only home can offer, usually.

As the check engine light lit up on to the dashboard, I ignored it and pulled into the garage, saving the exploration of that for another day. I had seven messages on my answering machine, and the flicking red light looked to me like a bomb ready to go off.

I opted for a cup of tea and my couch before I

would look at the mail or check the messages. I spotted my Bible sitting on the table next to the couch and realized that I had not looked at my scripture for the day, a routine I keep most days. Having so much to accomplish that day and anxious to get started, I neglected to do so. So I picked it up, and this is what the Lord would have said to me on that day if I had taken the time to spend time with Him before I started the day:

> Therefore do not worry, saying, what shall we eat? Or what shall we drink? Or what shall we wear? For after all these things the Gentiles seek. For your heavenly Father knows that you need all these things. (Matthew 6:31–32)

There is not too much more to say.

41

HEROES

I heard a sermon recently that spoke about our biblical heroes. As I listened, a new light was shed on them that spoke to my spirit and fed my passion—family. Love of family and concern for legacy were also the concerns of these heroes, as well as their faith that set them apart to become our heroes.

Moses was sent out in a safe, comfortable basket by his family. Noah gathered his family in the ark. Isaac blessed Jacob and Esau. Jacob blessed Joseph and his brothers. Joseph forgave his brothers and then fed and sheltered them in his care. Rahab negotiated for her family and secured a safe place for them marked by a scarlet thread. Ruth walked beside her mother-in-law.

This set me thinking. Not that we should alter our prayers, but in this season when our concerns and prayers are focused on the country, government, the environment, and abortion (rightly so), let us not forget our loved ones. Put them in the basket, the boat, or the house and walk beside them. Let us cover them with blessings and place a scarlet thread over them.

> Be sober, be vigilant, because your adversary the devil walks about like a roaring lion, seeking whom he may devour. (1 Peter 5:8)

42

BE ENCOURAGED

So many prayer requests, problems, and concerns have been floating around this past week, dealing with marriages in crisis, employment issues, health, and decisions to make. That's life and all that surrounds it. It's good to reach out and ask for prayer, but also don't forget the importance of the word.

I am often asked to pray with someone or to keep them in prayer after they have shared their concern or problem. So overwhelmed with concern, I have no words for them. With only sympathy and compassion, I rely on the only help I can offer, the written word.

> Fear not, for I am with you. Be not dismayed, for I am your God. I will strengthen you. Yes, I will help you. I will uphold you with my righteous right hand. (Isaiah 41:10)

> The Lord will fight for you. And you shall hold your peace. (Exodus 14:14)

> For I, the Lord your God will hold your right hand. Saying to you, "Fear not, I will help you." (Isaiah 41:13)

These things I have spoken to you, that in me you may have peace; in the world you will have tribulation; but be of good cheer, I have overcome the world. (John 16:33)

Be encouraged today because our God is still in the business of parting the waters and holding your hand. Always take something away from the situation or problem you were faced with.

43

WALKING IN HIS GRACE

(Merriam-Webster Collegiate Dictionary) definitions of grace: Unmerited divine assistance given to humans for their regeneration or sanctification. A virtue coming from God. A state of sanctification enjoyed through divine assistance. God shows us His divine grace in His word.

> They refused to obey and they were not mindful of your wonders that you did among them. But they hardened their necks and in their rebellion they appointed a leader to return to their bondage, but you are God, ready to pardon, gracious and merciful. Slow to anger, abundant in kindness and did not forsake them. (Nehemiah 9:17)

That is divine grace. Amen.

As we approach spring, we get the urge to dig in our gardens and get out the window cleaner to rid our windows of winter's grime and let in some more sunlight. Also, this is a good time to dig into our minds and actions to clean out what might not be pleasing to our Father. Maybe we can let some sunshine in too. We will soon celebrate the resurrection of Jesus, the demonstration of God's power and love for us. Let's accept and walk in His grace as we prepare to receive the blessings this day holds for us.

But He, being full of compassion, forgave their iniquity, and did not destroy them. Yes, many a time He turned His anger away and did not stir up all His wrath. (Psalm 78:38)

For the Lord God is a sun and shield; The Lord will give grace and glory. No good thing will He withhold from those who walk uprightly. (Psalm 84:11)

And of His fullness we have all received, and grace for grace. For the law was given through Moses, but grace and truth came through Jesus Christ. (John 1:16–17)

44

RESURRECTION

My thoughts today were on the coming celebrations for Resurrection Sunday. The definition of *resurrection* is to revitalize or revive. I thought about all the things we might have let die in our lives and wondered if God didn't want us to resurrect them. Was it a desire, a dream, a purpose that God planted that died with fear or worry or just because we were too busy with other things?

I have been reading in Matthew for the past few days. The account gives the genealogy, biography, and characteristics of Jesus. It goes on to share His beliefs and instances of his healing and coming into relationships with people. The last chapter explains His purpose and instruction to the church, which is us.

> Teaching them to observe all things that I have commanded you; and lo, I am with you always, even to the end of the age. Amen. (Matthew 28:20)

So let's ponder what is dead. What needs a revival? How can we fertilize and water our purpose so we can fulfill the command to add to the kingdom and give testimony of our victories? The gospel of Matthew gives us the credentials of Jesus our teacher. His words will guide us. His power and authority were seen and recorded. He is on board to do His part. Jesus, tell us our part.

> Ask, and it will be given to you, seek, and you will find, knock, and it will be opened to you. (Matthew 7:7)

> Again, I say to you that if two or more agree on earth concerning anything that they ask, it will be done for them by My Father in heaven. (Matthew 18:19)

Blessed Resurrection Sunday and beyond.

45

SPRINGTIME

There's no rhyme or reason to it, but this year's spring is looking so bright o me. The different shades of green dotted with pink and white flowers span the roadsides. It seems to me this all appeared quickly overnight. I know that God demonstrates in the natural what is being done in the spirit, so I thought about what I was seeing and what God was saying. On Sunday while I was at a spirit-filled worship service, a precious sister in the Lord leaned over and said to me and the young lady seated next to me, "I believe this is for you. I feel the Lord saying even the sunflowers turn to the heavens." Sunflowers being one of my favorite flowers, I received that and turned to the word of God to find answers to what I was seeing and feeling this spring.

> For lo, the winter is past. The rain is over and gone. The flowers appear in the earth. The time of singing has come, and the voice of the turtledove is heard in our land. (Song of Solomon 2:11–12)

> So why do we worry about clothing? Consider the lilies of the field, how they grow, they neither toil nor spin, and yet I say to you that even Solomon in all his glory was not arrayed like one of these. Now if

God so clothes the grass of the field, which today is, and tomorrow is thrown into the oven, will He not much more clothe you, O you of little faith? (Matthew 6:28–30)

Then He who sat on the throne said, "Behold, I make all things new." And He said to me, "Write, for these words are true and faithful." (Revelation 21:5)

That about said it all for me. We have hope after the winter of trial and provision for our needs. He will fix it and make things new. It was a reminder of faith in His word that He is true and faithful.

Did the spring speak to you this season? Did you breathe it in? As the sunflower looks to the heavens for it growth and provision, so shall we.

46

OUR TESTIMONY

And they overcame him by the blood of the Lamb and the word of their testimony. And they did not love their lives to the death. (Revelation 12:11)

After reading that verse, I began to think about how important our testimony is. It can overcome and defeat the enemy. That is awesome and powerful. It may be just a few words, a lot of words, or maybe an action. I like to think of it as a knockout punch. If we think about it, we all have a testimony. It might be a little thing or a big thing, but it all throws a punch in the right direction. If you are walking and talking, you have a testimony. Share it in a conversation. Pray for an open door so you can share it.

If you have a voice, you can have the victory. If you have breath, you have business for the Lord. If you have a pulse, you need to serve a purpose for the Lord. Next time something seems like a coincidence, look for the hand of the Lord to be the one that arranged it. Look for the berry moments. Be obedient to the prompting of the spirit for there are blessings in obedience. Be prepared always.

> But, sanctify the Lord God in yours hearts, and always be ready to give a defense to everyone who asks you for a reason for the hope that is in you, with meekness and fear. (1 Peter 3:15)

47

RESTORED

A wealthy man was about to purchase a painting for one million dollars. As a collector of fine art, he had searched for the painting for years. Before the transaction was completed, both the seller and potential buyer agreed to put the painting on display so the public could view and appreciate its beauty. Somehow, while the seller was pointing out the fine points of the painting, he slipped off the stage and grabbed onto the easel on which the painting was perched. The painting was severely damaged, much to the horror of all who were present and had witnessed the unfortunate accident. The seller vowed to have the painting restored, and it was expertly and beautifully done by experts in the field of restoration. The original buyer, still in awe over the beauty and valve of this painting, now offered two million dollars to buy it. "Why would you do that?" asked the press and all in the art world. His response was, "Because of the story that is attached to the painting. It's not just a lost painting that was found. Its value has increased because of the story that is now attached to it. It became more valuable after the restoration. It has a story."

My first thought after reading that was, *How much more valuable are we?* Yes, God had a plan for our lives. We messed up. Maybe we went off the path for a while or lingered in the pig pen for a while. Finally God got our attention, most likely with a shot to the head, and we got back to plan A with the help of the experts in the kingdom. Heaven is smiling, and there is joy in the house.

Let's take inventory today of what has gotten restored in our lives. Was it our bodies, our finances, our families, and probably so much more? We can't put a value on it. It is priceless because it has a story to go with it.

> He restores my soul, he leads me in the paths of righteousness for his name sake. (Psalm 23:3)

I am sure you have a story, a testimony. God always has a plan.

48

DIVINE APPOINTMENT

Recently I was asked to go along to doctor appointments with close friends who needed an extra ear to listen to the test results and possible treatments for their medical situations. These appointments somehow led into God conversations with the doctors. I do not know and may never know the end results or if our beliefs were accepted and acted on. I do know we planted seeds of our faith, and these precious souls were added to our prayers.

> … that Christ may dwell in your hearts through faith; and that you being rooted and grounded in love, may be able to comprehend with all the saints what is the breadth and length and height and depth, and to know the love of Christ which surpasses knowledge, that you may be filled up to all the fullness of God. (Ephesians 3:17–19)

Certainly these were divine appointments orchestrated by God—the times, the places, the words. He directs our steps, and if we can sense the leading of the Spirit, we obey and accomplish His works. I like to believe that the parking spot closest to the store I am going into is also a divine appointment, especially when my legs are tired, and that the sale item I need will still be on the shelf. Like berries, those small, sweet things, we experience divine appointments orchestrated from above every day.

49

PRODIGALS

I listened to a different viewpoint of the scripture about the prodigal son. It's a familiar story about a son who runs off with his inheritance and lives a life away from all he was taught. Meanwhile, his brother is faithful to all the teachings and truths he was taught. When the prodigal son wants to return home and repent, his brother is not too happy and questions why he should be treated so well. He proceeds to list all the reasons that all the merry making and feasting in honor of his brother was not fair.

> But he was angry and would not go in. Therefore his
> father came out and pleaded with him. (Luke 15:28)

Most prodigals are welcomed home with open arms and feasting. I know that's what happens in heaven. The Father is delighted just as the father in the gospel of Luke. Brother number two might also be a different kind of prodigal. He can't forgive or love, and he turns away from the inheritance his heavenly father has for him. Its two prodigals, two different stories.

50

RESET AND REBOOT!

As I was watering my indoor plants this morning and picking off the dead leaves, I decided to give them a shot of fertilizer to stimulate some new growth. I thought how we also, as living, growing beings, might need some fertilizer from time to time. We need something to reboot and reset our spirits.

Definitions of *reboot* and *reset* include to restart, to gain anew, and to renew. Maybe it is time for a reboot. Maybe we are experiencing a loss of hope, unbelief, or fear. It's time to reboot, to fertilize. After all, we are the branches.

> I am the vine and you are the branches. He who abides
> in Me, and I in Him, bears much fruit; for without Me
> you can do nothing. (John 15:5)

Let's pick off the dead branches and leaves. Let's reboot, reset. Pick up the Bible and read the word. Put on worship music in your home and car. Connect with a community of believers. Reset and fertilize the branches so the vine may prosper. Happy gardening.
Look for the berries.

51

KEEP YOUR EYES OPEN

Some days, so many cares and concerns invade our minds that we become overwhelmed with worry and fear. One of my devotionals this week brought me to a story about Elisha and one of his servants. The servant woke one morning to find an army surrounding the city with horses and chariots. The servant said to Elisha, "Alas my master! What shall we do?" Sounds like us in our prayer closets. I know we know better, but when concerns and worries are so many, so immediate, so needing a quick answer, fear sets in. This was Elisha's response:

> So he answered, "Do not fear, for those who are with us are more than those who are with them." And Elisha prayed, and said, "Lord, I pray open his eyes that he may see." Then the Lord opened the eyes of the young man, and he saw. And behold, the mountain was full of horses and chariots of fire all around Elisha. So when the Syrians came down to him Elisha prayed to the Lord and said, "Strike this people, I pray, with blindness": And He struck them with blindness according to the words of Elisha. (2 Kings 6:16–18)

My prayer today is for you and me to see in the spirit, to be able to see with our spiritual eyes this huge army from God that surrounds our every concern, every worry, every need, and every situation. If God is for us, who can be against us?

52

PRIMARY ENEMIES

Some primary enemies affect all of us at various times in our lives. One is anxious fear, another is rejection, and still another is lonely isolation. And how about self-loathing? Count it all an enemy of our soul and our journey. Beware; take heed. Remember to stick to the battle plan. In those times, read the word. Worship, or if you can, just put on a Christian CD. Stay connected to church and community.

Above all, be still in spirit and mind. You would not tell your surgeon who is getting ready to operate on you how to perform the surgery. The same goes for our spiritual surgeon who is getting ready to do something in our lives, something the enemy doesn't want to happen. Trust your God to know how to solve the problem. Let Him have his way. The Bible gives us the direction in which to proceed against those attacks that come to all of us.

> Be still, and know that I am God. I will be exalted among the nations, I will be exalted in the earth The Lord of hosts is with us. The God of Jacob is our refuge. (Psalm 46:10–11)

God bless and stay strong.

53

ANCIENT WELLS

I listened to a sermon this Sunday about wells. Isaac dug a well that he named Rehoboth. I recently visited family in Delaware very near Rehoboth, a beach area in Delaware. I have learned to discern when God is speaking and the Holy Spirit is prompting me to do something. So I opened the Bible to see what the word of God had to say about wells and water.

Wells, it seems, symbolize a healthy, prosperous community. Isaac was prosperous and blessed because of the wells that were dug by his father Abraham's servants. The Philistines envied this and told Isaac to leave, fearful of his power and wealth. Isaac decided to again open the wells that the Philistines had filled in with earth. When the precious water is again found, the local herdsmen claimed it as their water, and Isaac was forced to open other wells, causing quarrels over the water rights. When he came to the well that caused no quarrel, he named it Rehoboth.

> And the Lord appeared to him the same night and said, "I am the God of your father Abraham, do not fear, for I am with you. I will bless you and multiply your descendants for my servant Abraham's sake." (Genesis 26:24)

"A woman of Samaria came to draw water. Jesus said to her, 'Give Me a drink'" (John 4:7). She responded, "Are you greater than our father Jacob, who gave us the well, and drank from it himself, as well as his sons and his livestock?" (John 4:12).

Isaac's son Jacob had inherited the well, and it was still flowing with life-sustaining water. It was a deep well. The woman soon found out just who Jesus is. Jesus came to the well to use it for salvation, light, wisdom, and knowledge. He dug it a little deeper. The well gave living water and spread through the village.

Let's go dig our wells again, wells that the enemy is trying to fill up with dirt and plug. What's in our legacy that will quench our thirst for light, peace, wisdom, and knowledge? Maybe it is the cloud of witness in the world or our own family of God and church. We need to dig up what has been given to us through the legacy that has been left to us. It may take a few attempts, but like Isaac we will succeed and receive the blessings of Abraham. We also put the fear of God in our enemies when we dig in our wells and find the blessings that are there.

Who needs a shovel?

54

ANCESTRY WITH GOD

Who am I? I think at one time or another we have all asked that question. So I thought it would be interesting to see what the Bible had to say about it.

> And the Lord will make you the head and not the tail. You shall be above only and not be beneath. If you heed the commandments of the Lord your God which I command you today, and are careful to observe them. (Deuteronomy 28:13)

> You are the light of the world. A city set on a hill cannot be hidden. (Matthew 5:14)

> When I call to remembrance the genuine faith that is in you, which dwelt first in your grandmother Lois and your mother Eunice, and I am persuaded is in you also. (2 Timothy 1:5)

Walk in that today and be blessed.

55

PRAYER

I have always stood in awe when some of God's people pray with such eloquence and flow of words. I do not have that gift, and yes, it is a gift. I find myself praying silently when in a group. One beautiful Sunday morning while driving to church, I was thanking God for the bright shine of the sun; the clouds and sky aligned to create puffy figures that triggered the imagination. I suddenly felt a peace and a knowing that I was praying and my prayers were being heard. I continued out loud with my prayer list as if I was having a conversation with the barista at a coffee shop. Clearly, God hears no matter how we communicate with Him.

> Blessed be the Lord, because He has heard the voice of my supplications! The Lord is my strength and shield: My heart trusts in Him. And I am helped. Therefore my heart greatly rejoices and with my song I can praise Him. (Psalm 28:6–7)

> Lord, in trouble they have visited You, They poured out a prayer when Your chastening was upon them. (Isaiah 26:16)

It shall come to pass that before they call, I will answer: and while they are still speaking, I will hear. (Isaiah 65:24)

And when you pray, you shall not be like the hypocrites. For they love to pray standing in the synagogues and on the corners of the streets, that they may be seen by men. Assuredly, I say to you, they have their reward. But you, when you pray, go into your room, and when you have shut your door, pray to your Father who is in the secret place; and your Father who sees in secret will reward you openly and when you pray, do not use vain repetitions as the heathen do. For they think that they will be heard for their many words. Therefore do not be like them. For your Father knows the things you have need of before you ask Him. In this manner, therefore, pray; Our father in heaven, Hallowed be your name. Your kingdom come. Your will be done on earth as it is in heaven. Give us this day our daily bread and forgive us our debts, as we forgive our debtors. And do not lead us into temptation, but deliver us from the evil one. For yours is the kingdom and the power and the glory forever, Amen. (Matthew 6:5–13)

Likewise the Spirit also helps in our weakness. For we do not know what we should pray for as we ought, but the Spirit Himself makes intercession for us with groaning which cannot be uttered. Now He who searches the hearts knows what the mind of the Spirit is because He makes intercession for the saints according to the will of God. (Romans 8:26–27)

… who in the days of His flesh, when He had offered up prayers and supplications, with vehement cries and tears to Him who was able to save Him from death, and was heard because of His godly fear. (Hebrews 5:7)

So what have we learned? God hears songs of prayer. God hears a whispered prayer, and God hears groaning prayer. It doesn't have to be too many words because He knows what the need is before we ask. He loves the obedience of prayer. He loves the honor it gives Him, and the expression of your faith in Him. Most of all He loves you taking the time to talk to Him. Listen for His voice for prayer is a conversation. Expect a reply. How will you pray today?

56

RANDOM THOUGHTS TO PONDER

Following are some statements to ponder. Early morning berries today.

Faith equals courage. There is head knowledge, and there is heart knowledge. When praying for deliverance for a person, pray against the spirit of addition, the spirit of infirmity, the spirit of pornography, the spirit of greed, the spirit of suicide.

What can't you live without? Is it something that lasts forever, or is it just for the moment?

"And he said to them, 'Take heed and beware of covetousness, for one's life does not consist in the abundance of the things he possesses.'" (Luke 12:15)

I am going to put these thoughts out there in case you want to ponder them while you are in traffic or on hold waiting for customer service to pick up.

- Revelation will bring you to preparation for His will.
- The Lord does not replace our sorrow; He transforms our sorrow into joy.

For some reason not known to me, today I close with Deuteronomy 30:15–16: "See, I have set before you today life and good, death and evil. In that I command you today to love the Lord your God, to walk in His ways, and to keep His commandments, His statutes, and His judgments, that you may live and multiply. And the Lord your God will bless you in the land which you go to possess."

57

IMPATIENCE

I heard the horn in the car behind me beep the very second the light changed. I changed lines in the grocery store three times when I felt the clerk was not moving fast enough. Maybe you had no patience to wait your turn for the phone inquiry you needed to make. Somebody got the message and initiated the call-back system, saying you can press 1 and get a return call when your turn comes. Or was the sermon too long? Did you start to shift in your seat and wonder when the point of the talk was coming? I started to wonder what God had to say about this. I went to the word and found what I share today.

> I would have lost heart, unless I believed that I would see the goodness of the Lord in the land of the living. Wait on the Lord. Be of good courage, and he shall strengthen your heart. Wait, I say, on the Lord! (Psalm 27:13–14)

> Rest in the Lord and wait patiently for Him; do not fret because of him who prospers in his way, because of the man who brings wicked schemes to pass. Cease from anger and forsake wrath. Do not fret; it only causes harm. For evildoers shall be cut off. But

those who wait on the Lord, they shall inherit the earth. (Psalm 37:7–9)

Eternal life to those who by patient continuance in doing good seek for glory honor and immortality. (Romans 2:7)

However for this reason I obtained mercy, that in me first Jesus Christ might show all longsuffering as a pattern to those who are going to believe on Him for everlasting life. (1 Timothy 1:16)

That you will not become sluggish, but imitate those who through faith and patience inherit the promises. (Hebrews 6:12)

The Lord is not slack concerning His promise, as some count slackness, but is longsuffering towards us. Not willing that any should perish but that all should come to repentance. (2 Peter 3:9)

Amazing how His word covers all things that concern us.

58

GOD IN OUR EVERYDAY

Did we leave God in church last Sunday? Maybe He is still in the car? No, I checked; He is not in the car. Seems He never made it out of service. The parking lot is jammed, and nobody is letting Sister Jill or Brother Jack into the lane heading for the exit. I know the pastor was a bit long today and everyone is in a rush to get some lunch, but let's get this line moving.

Maybe it's time to take God out of the box—or should I say the pew—for a relationship beyond Sunday. It is what He truly would love, and His word tells us so. Do you ask Him for grace in an awkward worldly situation? Maybe for a parking space near the store you are going into on a cold winter day? How about before getting a haircut or shopping for that outfit for a special occasion? What about some godly favor on the job interview or the house or apartment you just put a bid on? Or maybe travel mercies before a road trip?

Here's what our Abba has to say.

> Unless the Lord had been my help, my soul would soon
> have settled in silence. (Psalm 94:17)

God the refuge of His people and conqueror of the nations. God is our refuge and strength. A very present help in trouble. (Psalm 46:1)

But the very hairs of your head are all numbered. Do not fear therefore, you are of more value than many sparrows. (Luke 12:7)

For with God nothing will be impossible. (Luke 1:37)

One God and Father of all who is over all and through all and in all. (Ephesians 4:6)

For you will not leave my soul in Hades. Nor will you allow your Holy One to see corruption. (Acts 2:27)

Does anyone need more help opening the box? Hallelujah! Let Him out.

59

A WORD FOR TODAY

Psalm 20 The Assurance of God's saving Work

May the Lord answer you in the day of trouble. May the name of the God of Jacob defend you. May He send you help from the sanctuary, and strengthen you out of Zion. May He remember all your offerings, and accept your burnt sacrifice. May He grant you according to your heart's desire, and fulfill all your purpose. We will rejoice in your salvation, and in the name of our God we will set up our banners! May the Lord fulfill all your petitions. Now I know that the Lord saves His anointed: He will answer him from His holy heaven with the saving strength of His right hand. Some trust in chariots, and some in horses: But we will remember the name of the Lord our God. They have bowed down and fallen; but we have risen and stand upright. Save, Lord! May the King answer when we call?

60

WAITING

It might be a long line at the store or holding on a phone line waiting for a customer agent to pick up. Waiting is not fun, and most of us don't want to do it. What if that wait is for a new job or a mate? Maybe it's for a prodigal child to return home or for healing of your heart or medical condition. What if the wait is so long that you give up, leave the long line, and hang up the phone?

This is what I found that God had to say in the word.

> But as for me, I trust in You, O Lord, I say you are my God. My times are in your hand; Deliver me from the hand of my enemies and from those who persecute me. (Psalm 31:14–15)

Trust is an attribute developed through remembering what God has done for you in the past. Maybe there were different circumstance, but He proved His power and faithfulness. So remember past victories.

> Let us not grow weary while doing good, for in due season we shall reap if we do not lose heart. (Galatians 6:9)

So there is a time for things to happen in your

favor. It's possible that others in God's plan need to get in line to complete what you are waiting for.

> Therefore humble yourself under the mighty hand of God, that He may exalt you in the due time, casting all your care on Him, because He cares for you. (1 Peter 5:6–7)

Keep doing what you are doing without stress and anxiety. Wait in joy, peace, and anticipation. As a nurse I have seen firsthand that stress can produce physical and medical conditions.

> For the vision is yet for an appointed time. But at the end it will speak, and it will not lie. Though it tarries, wait for it; because it will surely come, it will not tarry. (Habakkuk 2:3)

Let's settle in, brothers and sisters. Most appointments we have in the natural require waiting time. We are told to come early to complete paperwork. That happens in the spirit world too. Our paperwork in the spirit is to show up early and pray, keep calm, and trust. The appointment does happen, though it tarries.

61

EVEN THOUGH

As we approach Thanksgiving, I am reminded of a scripture in Habakkuk.

> Though the fig tree may not blossom, Nor fruit be on the vines; Though the labor of the olive may fail, and the fields yield no food; Though the flock may be cut off from the fold, and there be no herd in the stalls—Yet I will rejoice in the Lord, I will joy in the God of my salvation. The Lord God is my strength. He will make my feet like deer's feet, and He will make me walk on my high hills. (Habakkuk 3:17–19)

The prophet speaks about tough times on the way. Things might get worse before they get better. It sounds like some situations we might be in right now—loss of health or employment, the death of a loved one, or a devastating national disaster. There is a promise here that we can hold onto in this season of giving thanks. Another thought that has come to mind this day is one I hope speaks to us over and over again: God does not put us through the fire without purpose but to bring us out of bondage into relationship with Him. Give Him thanks for what you have and for what He has coming for you.

62

PONDERING

To *ponder* is "to think about something carefully, especially before making a decision or reaching a conclusion."

> But Mary kept these things, and pondered them in her heart. (Luke 2:19)

Following are more thoughts to ponder:

- You have to go into the darkness to shed and speak light. Light does not speak to light.
- God is not limited to time and space. He is the same yesterday, today, and forever.
- He hears all prayers, eloquent and simple.
- Worry equals fear and negates trust.

I am about to complete a study on the book of Isaiah. Knowing full well the many layers of this book that tell of truth and prophecy, I found these issues interesting.

- *God's MO (modus operandi):* He listens, speaks, and warns; if there is no response, He acts. He allowed the Israelites to be captives in Babylon, but eventually He allowed them freedom with instructions to repent, with promises that hold true today. The call, the promise, is for spiritual renewal, restoration of the temple, and obedience to His direction.

- *Relevance to today:* I will set you free if you turn your lives around and listen to my plan for peace and prosperity. Rebuild the church to represent my words and my plan. Restore your homes to godly principles.

But seek ye first the kingdom of God, and His Righteousness, and all these things shall be added unto you. (Matthew 6:33)

63

GOT MILK?

A popular commercial implies that if you have milk, you have what is necessary to make things better. You can't go through a winter storm without picking up milk. Your cookies will taste better with milk. Milk makes things happen. It makes puddings, cakes, and cheese; you can add it to some sauces; and don't forget ice cream. It builds muscles and mustaches. It expands and creates and adds. Today the Lord showed me what else expands, creates, and multiplies and can be added if we give what we have to Him.

> When it was evening, the disciples came to Him saying, "This is a deserted place, and the hour is already late. Send the multitudes away, that they may go into the villages and buy themselves food." But Jesus said to them, "They do not need to go away. You give them something to eat." And they said to Him, "We have only five loaves and two fish." He said, "Bring them here to me." (Matthew 14:15–18)

Bring them here to me. Jesus multiplied the five loaves and fish, fed multitudes, and had leftovers. What has God blessed you with? Is it money, time, service, gifts, wisdom, talents? He wants to expand it, create with it, and add to the kingdom work. Give Him the little you have, and He will multiply it, enhance it, and combine it with others who give of what they have. There will also be some left over. There is power in unity. You don't have to fix it or do it alone. We have more than milk. What do you have? *Bring them to Him.* He wants to show you what He can do. It might seem like a big undertaking that He has set before you. Step out and bring Him what you have.

64

PLANS

Recently, my daughter shared a text she had received concerning the world's view on setting life goals. I immediately thought, *Wow, talk about putting pressure on yourself.* I will give you the short version: graduate college at twenty-two, be married with kids at twenty-five, and you're your dream job at thirty. Funny, right? Life is not a race or a competition. How different God's plan is for our lives. As usual, His plan is opposite of the world's. Let's take a look at His plan.

> For I know the thoughts that I think toward you, says the Lord, thoughts of peace and not evil, to give you a future and a hope. (Jeremiah 29:11)

> To everything there is a season, A time for every purpose under heaven: A time to be born, and a time to die; A time to plant, and a time to pluck what is planted; A time to kill, and a time to heal; A time to break down, and a time to build up; A time to weep, and a time to laugh; A time to mourn, and a time to dance;
> Time to cast away stones, and a time to gather stones; A time to embrace, and a time to refrain from embracing; A time to gain, and a time to lose; A time to keep,

and a time to throw away; A time to tear, and a time to sew; A time to keep silence, and a time to seek; A time to love, and a time to hate; A time of war, and a time of peace. (Ecclesiastes 3:1–8)

A little one shall become a thousand, and a small one a strong nation. I the Lord will hasten it in its time. (Isaiah 60:22)

Having made known to us the mystery of Hiwill, according to His good pleasure which He purposed in Himself. (Ephesians 1:9)
What more could be said.

65

ISRAEL, THE JOURNEY

Last summer, I did a study on wells—the sources of water, both physical and spiritual. It started with a sermon I listened to about wells of living water. Jesus met with the Samaritan woman in the gospel of John, and she questions Jesus as to why He wants to drink water from a well given by their father Jacob. Jesus answers that He has water too, living water, and whoever drinks of it will never thirst again. I believe this is the well that Isaac dug again after the Philistines had stopped it up, the only well that did not cause disagreement of ownership. It is the well he named Rehoboth. He was fruitful and prosperous, and his children and cattle drank from the well. He surely must have passed it on to his son Jacob.

This summer I planned a visit with my nephew, who recently moved to Delaware. As he eagerly showed me the lovely areas surrounding his new home, I became aware of the road signs with directions to a beach named Rehoboth. As a believer in signs and wonders. I call this incident a berry—a sweet, little thing God sends us to remind us He is always speaking. I considered these signs and directions to Rehoboth as berries.

My church hosted an interfaith dinner in an attempt to connect with our brothers and sisters in our community and show love and support for one another with a common goal. We had a rabbi from Greenport; a Catholic priest from the shrine in Manorville, Our Lady of the Island; and a minster from Cutchogue.

Our team of ministers hosted this dinner. After a delightful evening of fellowship, the rabbi announced that an interfaith pilgrimage was being planned to the Holy Land. As they distributed the literature, I felt a surge of joy as I read they would be visiting Rehoboth, the birthplace of the rabbi. Berry number three. I was going to Israel, a desire I had held for many years. God speaks berries to me. He had spoken, and I heard.

"What brought you here, and how did you hear about our trip?" was the first question for all of us to answer at the first meeting concerning our trip to the Holy Land. I got to share this story. I leave at the end of the month and am looking forward to what lies ahead. I will share when I return. Until then, God bless and may His face shine upon you.

66

ISRAEL, THE JOURNEY, PART 2

I just returned from an interfaith pilgrimage to Israel. There were so many levels to this adventure that I had a hard time deciding what to share. I finally thought the most important thing was that which would encourage us and show us what God is doing in Israel. The interfaith aspect touched me, and I truly saw God's heart and will unfold.

In Magdala, the home of Mary Magdalene, an ancient synagogue was discovered during the construction of a retreat house. Scripture tells us Jesus preached in synagogues in this area, and it is believed to be where He encountered Mary, who was one of His first followers. We were given permission to enter the ruins, sit on the stone seats, and pray and worship. As part of a movement named the Abrahamic Renewal, we worshipped with a Catholic priest, a rabbi, and a sheikh and his wife. The emphasis of the movement is focusing on things we agree on in an effort toward peaceful existence, that the tent of meeting not be stone and mortar, or border or boundary, but mind and spirit.

As our journey continued, we visited the sites from north to south Tel Aviv to Eliat. On our last day, we drove from Eliat across the desert, south to north. This took the better part of four hours with the Egyptian border to our right in plain view. Our destination was an area called Rehoboth, a small town founded by Yemenite Jewish refugees dating back to the mid-1600s. Previously, Isaac had dug wells that the Philistines had filled with earth. He found one that was good and deep and called it Rehoboth. We finished our adventure with a music and food festival themed "From Egypt to Rehoboth," the route we had just traveled. Egypt was a narrow place, and Rehoboth was a wide, deep place. The drive we had just taken reflected the spiritual journey of the Israelites and hopefully us. To dig a well that is deep and wide and to dig deeper into God's word gives us living water, like what the Samaritan woman received at Jacob's well. I wondered if it was the same well Isaac had dug and left to Jacob.

> Are you greater than our father Jacob, who gave us this well and drank from it himself as well as his sons and his livestock? (John 4:12)

67

THE TENT OF MEETING

One of the interesting points I took away from my trip to Israel was a message from Rabbi Gadi. He often spoke of the Jews' exodus from Egypt and the God we worship together.

> Moses took his tent and pitched it outside the camp, far from the camp, and called it the tabernacle of meeting. And it came to pass that everyone who sought the Lord went out to the tabernacle of meeting which was outside the camp. (Exodus 33:7)

The tent of meeting, pitched by Moses outside the Israelite camp, was a place where people could talk to God and He would meet them there. There, Moses met with God and others to inquire of the Lord. God's presence was shown there by a pillar of cloud.

Are you anxious? Fearful? Hopeless? Yes, yes, yes. We have all felt these emotions at some time during this time of isolation and separation because of the current health crisis. Church services are cancelled, churches are closed, social events are put on hold or cancelled, family is not visiting, and neighbors are held at a distance. Let's go back to the tent of meeting as in the Old Testament. The Israelites were in the wilderness, the same as we sometimes feel going through this crisis.

Let not mortar or stone, boundaries or borders stop us from meeting with God. Our tent is our backyard, our quiet corner, our rocking chair. Our tent is the mind and spirit. So inquire of the Lord often. Bring Him your concerns, cry out for your needs and those of your family. Then embrace the stillness that surrounds you by the mandates given to us by our leaders. Be safe. Our God is the same God who met Moses in the tent outside the camp—the one and only who will meet with us in mind and spirit in our tent of meeting, wherever that might me.

68

TENT OF MEETING, PART 2

It seems that every day, as we live in this time of fear, the unknown, and a virus that seems to have come out of a science fiction film, a new tent of meeting emerges. Churches share services online that people can watch and worship with. We have conference calls with prayer groups and sermons on the Christian TV channels. I am thankful for every one of them as they allow us to stay on track and in touch with the only one who can get us through this unusual time, the only one who can bring the peace that is needed and the calm over the fear. Also, these devices keep us in touch with one another. We need one another in this time so we know we are not the only ones going through a tough time.

A few months ago I read about a practice in Zimbabwe that soon expanded to London and New York City. The concept was that, when enduring trauma, despair, or unemployment, you went to the friendship bench, a bench located in a quiet area. You can go there to talk to "grandmothers" who are trained to listen to people struggling with depression or loss of hope, known in the Zimbabwean language as "thinking too much." This week I got a call from a neighbor who was thinking too much, so to maintain the practice of social distancing, we met at the bus stop bench at the end of my block. I immediately recalled the article about the friendship bench. I thought, *God, you are so faithful to provide another way to keep in touch, another way to give you the glory.* Before I knew it, we were in a conversation that brought healing, warmth, understanding, and hope. In this time of thinking too much, may we all find a friendship bench. If no one is around to meet with you, go anyway because you will find God there waiting to listen. Take a walk and find a bench—it's the new tent of meeting, a place to seek God either alone or through a friend. Stay safe and stay in touch.

69

THE VEIL IS TORN

More than ever before it is important to remember that the veil is torn, and there is fear, uncertainty, and worry in the world and in our spheres of contact. I shared in previous posts that the tent of meeting is not in brick and mortar or in boundaries or borders; it is in the minds and spirits of the faithful. In this holy time of Passover and Easter, let us remember the power of the blood. God in His wisdom is reminding us.

> Then, behold the veil of the temple was torn in two
> from top to bottom and the earth quaked, and the rocks
> were split. (Matthew 27:51)

The veil was not partially torn; it was torn all the way to make sure the way to Him was now completely open—not halfway but all the way. He was making sure we would understand that we can be in His presence anytime, anyplace, anywhere we want. He is only a prayer away. We will not celebrate in our places of worship in this holiest of seasons, but God is showing us in this difficult season that we will be with Him, worship Him, and put our requests before Him. Why? Because He is always there.

As we are quarantined to our homes, we know from scripture that we can access the throne as we pray for safety for ourselves and our families. Again, we need to go to the scriptures.

> Come my people enter your chambers, and shut up your doors behind you. Hide yourself as it were, for a little moment until the indignation is past. (Isaiah 26:20)

> Therefore the Lord will wait, that He may be gracious to you. Therefore He will be exalted, that He may have mercy on you. For the Lord is a God of justice. Blessed are those that wait for Him. (Isaiah 30:18)

Be blessed in this season of hope and renewal as we wait on the Lord.

70

GRIEF AND FORTY DAYS

As we approach our thirty-something day on lockdown, I am reminded of all the forty-day events in the Bible: forty years for the wilderness journey, forty days of Moses on the mountain receiving the Ten Commandments, Jesus's being tempted for forty days and forty nights in the desert. These are just random thoughts about what God is up to as we approach our forty days of isolation. What I do see from scripture is that change had always taken place after the forty days. I wonder how we will come out of this experience.

So how are we doing in our isolation? is the question. In the beginning, I would have said pretty well. We all are willing to do our part to combat this virus plaguing our world. As time passes, we begin to wonder if and when this time of waiting will pass. Anxiety, fear, loss of patience, doubt, and depression arise. The Israelites chose another way to deal with all those feelings while they were waiting for Moses to return from his forty days on the mountain. That did not work out well for them. When Moses saw that they were out of control and had resorted to another god, a manmade god, he became exceedingly angry.

Then Moses stood in the entrance of the camp and said. "Whoever is on the Lord's side come to me!" and all the sons of Levi gathered themselves together to him. (Exodus 32:26)

They chose the right God. As our patience runs out and our anxiety and depression move in, let us choose the right God. This experience of isolation is similar to the experience of loss, which produces grief. We lost our freedom, finances, familiar ways of life, routines, and in some cases so much more. Let us not lose our way to the only one who has all the answers to our questions and concerns. Let us not lose the ability to set before the throne of God all our concerns and, more importantly, to leave those concerns there.

As we grieve our losses, remember that it's okay to have a meltdown. In fact, it's *good* to have a meltdown. Cry it out for as long and as loudly as you need.

> For His anger is but for a moment, His favor is for life. Weeping may endure for a night but joy comes in the morning. (Psalm 30:5)

Grief is the product of unmet expectations. We expected to go on as normal and complete our plans, hopes, and dreams. Remember that grief comes in stages and waves to give us relief between feelings. It gives us time, a break, to see things differently and to regroup our thoughts. It gives us time to heal and hope again.

> But those who wait on the Lord shall renew their strength; They shall mount up with wings like eagles, They shall run and not be weary, They shall walk and not faint. (Isaiah 40:31)

71

BLOOMING TREES

At our last Sunday service—yes, via teleconference—we were given a scripture to meditate on for the week. I felt it was so appropriate because of the days and days of rain we were having. The rainy days had high winds and torrential downpours, as if there were an urgency to their mission of watering the earth. The scripture comes from the book of Hosea.

> Come, and let us return to the Lord; for He has torn, but He will heal; he has stricken, but He will bind us up. After two days he will revive us; on the third day He will raise us up that we may live in His sight. Let us know, let us pursue the knowledge of the Lord. His going forth is established as the morning; He will come to us like the rain, like the latter and former rain to the earth. (Hosea 6:1–3)

This week I received a newsletter from a missionary family serving in Jordan. They recently moved into a home that better serves their two young children and their ministry needs. This winter was particularly harsh for them because of the weather, loss of a parent, coworkers, health issues, and of course the shutdown due to the virus. I am sure we can all relate to that. When they were finally able to breathe and complete their move, they noticed that the almond trees that surround their home were in bloom. Obviously, the trees had not been damaged in the harsh winter and were budding. I was touched by a scripture they shared in that newsletter.

> Moreover the word of the Lord came to me saying, "Jeremiah, what do you see?" And I said, "I see a branch of the almond tree." Then the Lord said to me, "You have seen well, for I am ready to perform my word." (Jeremiah 1:11–12)

I began to look at the tree outside my living room window, an apple tree. Sure enough, the significant spring rains had produced buds and some green leaves on its branches. The same day, later in the afternoon, I received a video from my daughter who lives in Georgia. She was sharing a message with her church family online, something we all are taking part in during these days of isolation. I noticed she was sitting outside and behind her were rows and rows of pecan trees; they were all in full bloom because of the difference in weather. I felt the Lord was talking. From branch to bud to full bloom, slowly, patiently, hope abounds and the words from Hosea come alive: "He will heal us, He will bandage us up." The spring rains produce buds, leaves, fruit, and the fulfillment of His word as spoken to Jeremiah. "You have seen well, I am ready to perform my word. Lots to ponder—almonds, apples, pecans, and rain.

72

THE MEANING OF DREAMS

I have always had an interest in dreams and their meaning. I did a study on dreams in the Bible and their symbolic meanings. I also read a variety of books that shared various thoughts on Christian dream interpretation. I find the subject interesting as it is one of the ways that God speaks to us. I want to share what I found and an experience I had. I am believing God wants us to know something more about dreams.

The Bible records twenty-one dreams: ten in Genesis, one in Judges, one in Kings, three in Daniel, and six in Matthew. Some of them are clear warnings, while others predicted future events that are not yet seen to this day. A few were not clear but had symbolic features. We know God still speaks through dreams because "He is the same, yesterday, today and forever" (Hebrews 13:8).

Young Joseph had a dream. Though symbolic, it revealed that one day Joseph would rule over his brothers and have authority over them. In his dream, he and his brothers were gathering sheaves of wheat. After binding them stood, Joseph's stood up tall and erect, while his brothers' lay flat. He took pleasure in bragging and shared the dream. As sibling rivalry goes way back to Cain and Abel, it was alive and well in the land where Joseph lived, Canaan. Joseph's brothers, not too fond of Joseph because he was the favorite child, devised a plan to eliminate him. Reuben convinced his brothers that killing Joseph was not the best way. Instead he determined to sell him to a passing caravan going to Egypt. They got some pocket money and told their father Joseph had been eaten by a wild animal and only his multicolored coat was left. Typical sibling move: "We didn't do it." Later, we read that he ended up in Egypt and endured many trials, but he succeeded and became highly esteemed in the land.

> Now Joseph was governor over the land, and it was he who sold to all the people of the land. And Joseph's brothers came and bowed before him their faces to the earth. (Genesis 42:6)

Joseph's dream manifests in the natural.

Another Joseph had a dream given by God. Mary was betrothed to him, but rumor has it that she is with child. Not wanting to enter into a situation that would cause much gossip in the small village of Nazareth, Joseph prepared to break off the engagement. But he received a dream that instructed him to marry and support Mary because of the divine calling they had and the destiny of the baby. Dutifully, he did, preventing Mary from becoming a single parent. The next five dreams guided and clearly directed the birth and early years of Jesus. The magi, after visiting the newborn babe, were warned in a dream to return to their homes by a different route. Joseph and Mary were directed to Egypt to avoid Herod's decree to kill all the babies. In the next dream, Joseph and Mary were informed that Herod was dead and they could safely go back to Nazareth. They were cautioned, though, and reminded that Herod's son was now in power, so the dream conveyed that they should take the back way to avoid any leftover decrees. All clear directions.

A dream with clear direction is a dream that speaks to the inner person, your spirit. You respond to the clear direction because you know it is the right thing to do. When the dream is prophetic with symbols, you wait, pray, and ask what it means. Usually it's a desire God puts deep in your spirit, often unspoken. If and when it manifests in the natural, you then can say it was a true prophetic word spoken through a dream to you. It was prophecy. Dream, ask, pray, and believe. Manifestation equals prophetic dream.

Let's look at Gideon, a mighty man of God. He was raised to fight the Midianites, but he was scared, unsure of his ability to subdue this huge army. He decided to try to get an edge on the battle by spying on them in hopes of hearing their battle plan. What he did hear was two guys talking about a dream one of them had about a loaf of barley bread rolling through their camp, knocking down their tents, and defeating them. They believed this meant they were going to lose the fight. Well, Gideon went on to win the battle and defeat the Midianites. He overheard a prophetic dream.

This is a true story about a young family member who will remain unnamed. Decision making time was at hand, and her future was not quite clear; she was not sure which way to go. Decisions for her future were to be made by other parties. In her first dream, she was eating a delicious sandwich. In the second, she was ordering her favorite coffee and having a pleasant conversation with the server in another language. She asked me, "What do you think about these dreams? Any clue?" My reply was, "I think they are positive dreams. Remember to tuck your dreams away until they manifest in the natural so then you will know they were prophetic."

Between you and me, I believe those dreams were prophetic. I believe God is in this and she will get the unspoken desire of her heart. It is God who puts the desire in us in the first place. I can't say a word to the young woman until it manifests in the natural. I will wait and pray.

Taste and see that God is good. (Psalm 34:8)

More than a month passed, and she finally got an answer—yes! The path had opened. The details were cleared to open a way to the road ahead for her. The unspoken desire had manifested above and beyond.

And it shall come to pass afterward that I will pour
out my spirit on all flesh; Your sons and daughters

shall prophesy, Your old men shall dream dreams, your young men shall see visions. (Joel 2:28)

Praise God! Thank you, Jesus, from me and my young family member.

You will show me the path of life. In your presence is fullness of joy. At your right hand are pleasures forevermore. (Psalm 16:11)

73

THE POOL AT BETHESDA

On my recent interfaith trip to Israel, I learned some interesting facts that spoke to my spirit. Father Roy, a Catholic priest, was one of our leaders who contributed often to add to our tour guides' knowledge of the sites we were visiting. He pointed out a church that was built on the site of the home of Mary's mother, Anne, Jesus's grandmother. The home stood directly across the road in direct sight of a pool. The name of the church is St. Anne. I was particularly interested in this because I heard of the saint as someone I was named after. My mother had a difficult miscarriage prior to having me that almost caused her to lose her life. Being Catholic, she prayed to St. Anne, the patron saint of labor and delivery. She vowed that if she lived and ever became pregnant again, she would name the child Anne. That would be me.

As a group, we visualized Jesus coming to visit his grandmother many times in the years he was growing up. He must have witnessed the scene that occurred at the pool at Bethesda in certain seasons when an angel of the Lord went down into the pool and stirred the waters. Scripture tells us that there was a multitude of those who were blind, sick, lame, and withered waiting to be healed. When the time for His ministry was to unfold, Jesus walked over to the one man he appeared to know. Jesus saw him lying there and knew he had been there for a long time in that condition.

When Jesus saw him lying there, and knew that he already had been in that condition a long time, He said to him, "do you want to be made well?' The sick man answered Him, "Sir I have no man to put me into the pool when the water is stirred up, but while I am coming, another steps down before me." Jesus said to him, "Rise, take up your bed and walk." And immediately the man was made well, took up his bed, and walked. And that day was the Sabbath. (John 5:6–8)

Get off the merry-go-round. Someone or something is not getting you healed, delivered, or saved or giving you your breakthrough. If you have to, squirm, crawl, or wiggle to get into the pool. If you have to, walk in repentance, walk in prayer, walk in fasting, walk in humility, or walk in belief and get into the pool. Most important, get up and walk and take whatever you have been relying on to keep you from walking. Destroy it because you won't be needing it anymore. Get off your pallet.

You might want to pick up some walking shoes.

74

TIPS FROM ABOVE

Some thoughts have been floating around in my mind and quiet time these past two weeks that I feel led to share. One of my favorite preachers, the late David Wilkerson, left some messages that speak to our world today. His message on prayer spoke to me.

> So I say to you, ask, and it will be given to you, seek
> and you will find, knock and it will be opened to you.
> (Luke 11:9)

The Holy Spirit was given to us on our day of salvation. He is present with us. Now we have to ask for more of Him and for Him to walk with us in the current situation. Let's give Him quality time and space to enhance our walk and do His will to guide and direct us.

> You are of God, little children, and have overcome
> them, because He who is in you is greater than he who
> is in the world. (1 John 4:4)

This week my family and friends were presented with a host of concerns—some unique, some a return of the familiar that the enemy likes to unleash. Fresh revelation is so desperately needed.

I was asked to pray for these concerns. God, being the faithful God He is, provided, and I am delighted to share a testimony. When the battle begins and the trial is fresh and heavy, the waves of pain and confusing thoughts abound, and the road is not clear. The first prayer that goes up is that of "give me," "help me," "make a way," and "take the problem away." This is natural, but we often do not fully believe that He can do it. As the concerns increase and the problem gets bigger, we have to put on the full armor. The battle gets bigger, and the armor needs a boost.

The prayer must change to one of belief. Don't hold back the praise until the answer arrives; that's the wrong side. Praise as if you already have the answer. Pray the prayer of authority. We pray that it is done and needs to be released, the prayer of thanks before we see the result, and the prayer that blesses our faith in Him that all things are possible—the prayer of belief.

> But Jesus looked at them and said to them, "With men this is impossible, but with God all things are possible."
> (Matthew 19:26)

I testify to you today that I applied all of the above to three unrelated situations this week, and all three were turned around for victory. The revelation is not new. It may have been lost. It's up for renewal. Let us speak and pray and testify from fresh manna. God bless and may we take a stand and a posture of belief in all our concerns as they are brought into the throne room with Thanksgiving and praise.

75

ISAIAH

I started reading the major prophets and came upon these scriptures:

> Behold, the Lord makes the earth empty and makes it waste, Distorts it surface and scatters abroad its inhabitants. (Isaiah 24:1)

> The city of confusion is broken down. Every house is shut up, so that none may go in. (Isaiah: 24:10)

Then I went on to search the scriptures that were suggested in the commentary.

> Therefore her plagues will come in one day, death and mourning and famine. And she will be utterly burned with fire, for strong is the Lord who judges her. The kings of the earth who committed fornication and lived luxuriously with her will weep and lament for her when they see the smoke of her burning. Standing at a distance for fear of her torment, saying alas, alas, that great city Babylon, that mighty city, for in one hour your judgement has come. And the merchants of the earth

will weep and mourn over her for no one buys their merchandise anymore. Merchandise of gold and silver, precious stones and pearls, fine linen and purple silk and scarlet, every kind of citron wood, every kind of object of ivory, every kind of object of most precious wood, bronze, iron and marble and cinnamon and incense, fragrant oil and frankincense, wine and oil, fine flour and wheat, cattle and sheep horses and chariots and bodies and souls of men. The fruit that your soul longed for has gone from you and all the things that are rich and splendid have gone from you and you shall find them no more at all. The merchants of these things, who became rich by her, will stand at a distance for fear of her, weeping and wailing. Saying, alas, alas that great city that was clothed in fine linen purple, and scarlet, and adorned with gold and precious stones and pearls, for in one hour such riches came to nothing. Every ship master, all who travel by ship, sailors, and as many as trade on the sea, stood at a distance and cried out when they saw the smoke of her burning saying, what is like this great city? (Revelation 18:8–18)

As I was reading this part of scripture, I realized how very detailed the scripture is. It talked about everything necessary for survival—clothing, building materials, food, transportation, money, travel, and—the most profound—the loss of bodies and souls of men. God knew, and He was sending a message.

And now I have told you before it comes, that when it does come to pass you may believe. (John 14:29)

If my people who are called by My name will humble themselves and pray and seek My face, and turn from their wicked ways, then I will hear from heaven and forgive their sins and heal their land. (2 Chronicles 7:14)

76

LEVIATHAN THE MONSTER

May those curse it who curse the day, Those who are ready to arouse Leviathan. (Job 3:8)

Job was speaking about the day he was born. He was calling on those who cast spells on people and things to curse the day he was born, and they were the same ones who were prepared to rouse Leviathan. Who is Leviathan? My study proved this was not a good thing; it was an evil spirit. What a painful time Job was going through. His loss was unimaginable, and he was devastated to the point of wishing he were never born. We know that, when going through a difficult trial, we seek out explanations and answers other than those of God. Job was no different. I went a little deeper in my study of this spirit. *Webster's Dictionary* describes Leviathan as a sea monster defeated by Yahweh. In addition, it is described as a totalitarian state having vast bureaucracy, a politician state; something large and formidable, inspiring fear, powerful, intense, and capable. The Bible refers to this spirit as a beast. The Hebrew root word for *Leviathan* is *coiled* or *twisted*.

Job's trial continued as he tried to understand what had happened. Friends were no help, and his wife told him to curse God and die. God showed up in the storm with wisdom and direction. Recognizing Leviathan as the spirit attacking Job, He described the power the spirit had. God knew everything Job was going through had the power of a Leviathan spirit. God continued to tell Job of the power of this spirit, describing it as a monster.

> He beholds every high thing, He is king over all the children of pride. (Job 41:34)

Essentially, God was saying, "Job, you cannot fight and gain the victory without me." We all know the end of the story, and it's a good ending. I could not help but think about what is going on now, today, in 2020 in our world, our country, our homes, our stories, and our trials. I feel like that spirit has been loosed here in this day, in this time—so powerful, so strong, so disruptive. Scripture says that when he raises himself up, people are bewildered. Should we take a stand, become the brass wall, seek God, and pray to stand against the spirit of Leviathan? Maybe we need to show God that we are worthy of the victory He has planned. Let us not be bewildered. Oh, yes, we will win. Like Job, we have a good ending.

> In that day the Lord with His severe sword, great and strong, will punish Leviathan the fleeing serpent, Leviathan that twisted serpent; and He will slay the reptile that is in the sea. (Isaiah 27:1)

Webster's Dictionary got it right. Leviathan is a sea monster defeated by Yahweh in various scriptural accounts

77

SPECIAL FORCES OF HEAVEN

I was blessed this past February to visit Israel for a tour of the Holy Land. I might say I was also blessed to return home on the last flight out of Israel just before the worldwide pandemic exploded onto our land. Our tour guide was a special operations officer in the Israeli military. We all felt well taken care of both in the knowledge he shared of the holy sites as well as our security. At one point in our travel, another guide boarded our bus to conduct the tour of Bethlehem because our guide had been part of an operation there, so he might be recognized as a special forces officer and would not be welcome. We were glad to oblige the change of guides for this one tour.

I started to think of this elite group of people, special operations officers. In the background and undercover, they avert dangerous situations when alerted by the intelligence community. They set out to work to destroy the works of the enemy. Little or no recognition is given this team, nor do they want it. The plan of the enemy fails, doesn't come to pass, because of the actions of this elite fighting force. How awesome is this group of fighters. They face the enemy and destroy his plan.

In my devotion this morning, I was brought to Daniel 11:32: "Those who do wickedly against the covenant he shall corrupt with flattery, but the people who know their God shall be strong, and carry out great exploits."

> But those who wait on the Lord shall renew their strength, they shall mount up with wings like eagles, they shall run and not be weary, they shall walk and not faint. (Isaiah 40:31)

It all came together for me: these people are the intercessors of the world, the special forces of the spiritual realm. They wait upon the Lord. They are strengthened by His word. They hear from the intelligence source, the Holy Spirit, and stage the attack. They don't faint in battle. God's elite army works to avert the enemy's plan. They are in every corner of our world doing battle for what we may not know of. The General sits in the heavenly war room directing His troops.

Be encouraged—the Holy Spirit is at work directing the prayers of the intercessors around the world to avert what we may not know. They are God's special operations officers.

78

YOU PLEASE STAND

Is this what God is asking of us? Most likely you are facing more than one trial in your life right now. You are not alone On a bad day, we might say, "Enough is enough" and "I am not doing this anymore," like we have a choice. It is human nature to become depressed and anxious, wanting the problems to go away. Welcome to the rest of the world. How do we change this? What does God show us in His word, and more importantly what does God want us to do?

> And Samuel said to Jesse, "Are all the young men here?" Then he said, "There remains yet the youngest, and there he is keeping the sheep." And Samuel said to Jesse, "Send and bring him, for we will not sit down till he comes." (1 Samuel 16:11)

Samuel was running out of resources to kill Goliath, so he asked Jesse to send his youngest son, David, to go against the giant. He was going to stand and not sit down or back down from this situation that looked pretty hopeless. We all know the end of this story. To all, especially his brothers, it looked like it would not be a good end, but Samuel stood.

Ultimately, David brought down Goliath, the giant. God wants us to stand. He tells us how in His word.

> Therefore take up the full armor of God, so that you will be able to withstand in the evil day, and having done all, to stand. (Ephesians 6:13)

> And Jacob called unto his sons, and said, "Gather yourselves together, that I may tell you that which shall befall you in the last days." (Genesis 49:1)

> And men of all nations, from all the kings of the earth who had heard of his wisdom, came to hear the wisdom of Solomon. (1 Kings 4:34)

The Bible tells us how to stand: Put on the full armor. Ask for wisdom. Take on the mind of Christ. Hang out with people who have God's wisdom to share.

> Have I not commanded you? Be strong and of good courage; do not be afraid, nor dismayed, for the Lord your God is with you wherever you go. (Joshua 1:9)

79

ALL OF THE ABOVE

This is what I am feeling the Lord would like me to share today. Different scriptures and songs seemed to be coming to my attention for days, some through my daily devotional and some from television preachers and teachers. Also, some came from conversations with friends and relatives. Not all were related to anything, but all spoke a message. You have seen the "all of the above" option on a test or survey. It all has meaning and purpose, and that is the correct answer. All of the above.

"Great Is Your Mercy Towards Me" by Donnie McClurkin is a song that plays in my

head all day. It's a beautiful song and reminder of His love, kindness, mercy, and grace.

Below I share the scriptures that have come to me this last week or two over and over in all different situations. Take what pertains to what is going on in your mind and life and share the rest.

> But Jesus looked at them and said to them, "With men this is impossible, but with God all things are possible." (Matthew 19:26)

> Behold, the Lord's hand is not shortened, that it cannot save. Nor His ear heavy, that it cannot hear. (Isaiah 59:1)

I will put my spirit within you and cause you to walk in my statutes, and you will keep My judgments and do them. (Ezekiel 36:27)

For God has not given us the spirit of fear, but of power, and of love, and of a sound mind. (2 Timothy 1–7)

I was particularly grateful for that last scripture, for I felt that God was speaking a message. It was not some strange coincidence that was allowing these songs and scriptures to pop up repeatedly. I knew I had a sound mind that was given to me by God.

Be blessed in your coming and going. May you receive all of the above and count them as berries found along the way.

In the beginning was the Word, and the Word was with God and the Word was God. (John 1:1)

80

THE POWER OF TAKING AUTHORITY

If we could grab a hold of this power that has been given to us, we could use it for God and His kingdom as we strive to serve. In the book of Esther, we read how Queen Esther and Mordecai used their authority to establish the Feast of Purim after their victory over the schemes of Haman. Purim is a feast that celebrates victory with feasting, resting, and sharing food with one another.

> Then Queen Esther, the daughter of Abihail, and Mordecai the Jew wrote with full authority to confirm this second letter about Purim. And Mordecai sent letters to all the Jews, to the one hundred and twenty-seven provinces of the kingdom of Ahasuerus, with words of peace and truth, to confirm these days of Purim at their appointed time, as Mordecai the Jew and Queen Ester had prescribed for them, and as they had decreed for themselves and their descendants concerning matters of their fasting and lamenting. So the decree of Ester confirmed these matters of Purim and it was written in the book. (Esther 9:29–32)

Using their authority, their power, they established that feast and made it law; it is still practiced today as a reminder of the deliverance of the Jewish people from the enemy who came to kill, steal, and destroy.

> Where the righteous are in authority, the people rejoice, but when the wicked man rules, the people groan. (Proverbs 29:2)

> He taught them as one having authority, and not as the scribes. (Matthew 7:29)

> And they were astonished at His teachings, for His word was with authority. (Luke 4:32)

> Then He called His twelve disciples together and gave them power and authority over all demons, and to cure diseases. (Luke 9:1)

> Behold, I give you the authority to trample on serpents and scorpions, and over all the power of the enemy, and nothing shall by any means hurt you. (Luke 10:19)

This is us, folks. Authority releases power. And there's no better time than the present to embrace it. It seems it's not just one arrow being thrown but many coming from all different directions. That is how we know it's the enemy. Faith turns the arrows around. Taking authority over a situation releases power. No more defeated words or complaints—let us take our stand, tell the devil to leave because he has no place here, and make him close the door behind him on the way out. Take authority.

I love this scripture.

> But when Paul had gathered a bundle of sticks and laid them on the fire, a viper came out because of the heat, and fastened on his hand. So when the natives saw the creature hanging from his hand, they said to one another, "No doubt this man is a murderer, whom,

though he has escaped the sea, yet justice does not allow to live." But he shook off the creature into the fire and suffered no harm. (Acts 28:3–5)

I love that the snake goes back into the fire, and there is no harm done. The snake returns from where he came, the pit of fire. Don't forget the full armor. Let's try walking and thinking in authority today and every day. Let us also learn to shake it off.

81

ROMANS 16

This week as my morning study group reached the end of this amazing letter to the Romans written by the apostle Paul, I was drawn to these verses. I read them again and again and was sure the Lord would want me to share them and the revelation they hold with you. Paul had not yet visited Rome when he wrote this. The letter was intended to impart the teachings and establish the church as he was called to do. He sent his words and the promise of a future visit. He also introduced his friends who were going to minister to them. This is what caught my attention.

> Greet Priscilla and Aquila, my fellow workers in Christ Jesus, who for my life risked their own necks, to whom not only do I give thanks, but also all the churches of the Gentiles. Likewise greet the church that is in their house. Greet my beloved Epaenetus, who is the first fruits of Achaia to Christ. Greet Mary, who labored much for us. Greet Andronicus and Junias, my countrymen and my fellow prisoners, who are of note among the apostles, who also were in Christ before me. Greet Ampliatus, my beloved in the Lord. Greet Urbanus, our fellow worker in Christ, and Stachys my beloved. Greet Apelles, approved in Christ.

Greet those who are of the household of Aristobulus. Greet Herodion, my countryman. Greet those of the household of Narcissus, who are in the Lord. Greet Tryphaena and Tryphosa, who have labored in the Lord. Greet the beloved Persis, who has labored much in the Lord. Great Rufus, chosen in the Lord, and his mother and mine. Greet Asyncritus, Phelegon, Hermes, Patrobsd, Hermas and the brethren who are with them. Greet Philologus, and Julia, Nereus, and his sister, and Olympas and all the saints who are with them. (Romans 16:3–16)

My first thoughts were focused on the list of names—certainly a mixture of Greek and Jewish names and others common for slaves. In my search and study of this chapter, I found that twenty-six names are mentioned, and about one third are women. Tryphaena and Tryphosa were probably sisters and maybe even twins. Married couples were always mentioned together. There is no mention in my study that tells how Priscilla and Aquila risked their necks for Paul, but I would love to know. What about Rufus and his mother? Was she Paul's mom as well or a mother figure to him? Paul tells the Romans about his friends, kinsmen, countrymen, and fellow prisoners. I believe it might have been one of the first letters of recommendation ever. Paul also shared in this letter that his countrymen and fellow prisoners, who are of note among the apostles, were in Christ before him. These people had already accepted the Lord and were aware of the truth. Paul was surrounded by them as he pursued and had Christians imprisoned and killed. I have no doubt they were praying for him in earnest.

God prepared the way before Paul traveled on the Damascus road. This chapter spoke so clearly to me. Paul was not alone in his calling; God provided all he needed in abundance to accomplish the call on his life. He provided salvation to those saints before Paul's transformation. They were called to pray him in. A kinsman is a male relative, and countrymen are people residing in town or a nearby residence. Fellow prisoners are those who were fighting and praying for the same victory.

Let's us not doubt when called to do something for the Lord. Be confident that God has prepared the way. This chapter also revealed the power of a call to pray for our neighbors and relatives: God knows what He has in store for them and what part we are to play in His plan and purpose for them. Let us be encouraged and pray for one another. As Wilfred Grenfell said, "The service we render for others is really the rent we pay for our room on this earth."

82

TIME TO OPEN OUR EYES

There is not a day that goes by without hearing about another situation that needs prayer and God's help and intervention. Many days, the concerns are more than one. Some are immediate; others not so much. Discouragement abounds, faith falters, and fatigue sets in. Situations appear grave. But you are in a great place. You are in a place to let it go and let God. The reinforcements have arrived; the cavalry appears on the hills surrounding you.

In 2 Kings we read that the king of Syria was raging war against Israel. He sent his great army to find Elisha, the prophet, whom he believes was a spy in his palace. Elisha's servant spots the vast army descending upon them and alerts Elisha.

> And when the servant of the man of God arose early and went out, there was an army surrounding the city with horses and chariots. And his servant said to him, "Alas, my master! What shall we do?" So he answered, "Do not fear, for those that are with us are more than those that are with them." And Elisha prayed, and said, "Lord I pray, open his eyes that he may see." Then the Lord opened the eyes of the young man, and he saw. And behold,

the mountains were full of horses and chariots of fire all around. (2 Kings 6:15–17)

We don't have to do anything but pray and believe that the Lord has our concerns and situations under control. Pray that others open their eyes so that they may also see the help the Lord provides.

He is with us in the battle and in the fire. Lord, open our eyes that we may also see the armies and weapons that are greater than the enemies'. Let us not be discouraged or become fatigued as we battle with our concerns and trials. Lord, open our eyes that we may see you in our concerns, every ready to come and surround us with what we need to win the battle. Bring your horses and chariots of fire to surround us and overtake our enemies. Lord, open our eyes that we may see the berries.

83

SMOOTH STONES

The Philistines presented this big giant of a man, a champion to fight for the land in dispute. He was fully dressed in armor from head to toe and equipped with weapons of destruction. This giant was ready to do battle with any man the Israelites could get for a fight to the finish, winner takes all.

> Then David said to Saul, "Let no man's heart fail because of him, your servant will go and fight with this Philistine." (1 Samuel 17:32)

Saul agreed to let David fight and equipped him with full armor and weapons. David was not comfortable with the plan and shed the armor and weapons.

> Then he took his staff in his hand, and he chose for himself five smooth stones from the brook, and put them in a shepherd's bag, in a pouch which he had, and his sling was in his hand. And he drew near the Philistine. (1 Samuel 17:40)

Then David said to the Philistine, "You come to me with a sword, with a spear, and with a javelin. But I come to you in the name of the Lord of hosts, the God of the armies of Israel, whom you have defied." (1 Samuel 17:45)

David prevailed against the giant.

> Therefore David ran and stood over the Philistine, took his sword and drew it out of its sheath and killed him, and cut off his head with it. And when the Philistines saw that their champion was dead, they fled. (1 Samuel 17:51)

What can we take from this chapter? What did David have that we also need to defeat the enemy? The Lord rescued him from the lion and the bear. He had a revelation of God's power. He gave testimony of the power of God, and he had belief in God and His word. He took along his slingshot and five smooth stones to fling at the giant, which accomplished the win. I am sure that sometime in your journey you have said, "Thank God" for something God did for you and shared the experience. I have. We had revelation and testimony that produced belief. What do we have to fling at the giant? We have God's words. He is our rock, our smooth stone.

> *Stone 1:* And if it seems evil to you to serve the Lord, choose for yourselves this day whom you will serve, whether the gods which your fathers served that were on the other side of the river, or the gods of the Amorites, in whose land you dwell. But as for me and my house, we will serve the Lord. (Joshua 24:15)

> *Stone 2:* For the eyes of the Lord are on the righteous, and His ears are open to their prayers, but the face of the Lord is against those who do evil. (1 Peter 3:12)

> *Stone 3:* For the kingdom is the Lord's and He rules over the nations. (Psalm 22:28)

Stone 4: ... who delivered us from so great a death, and does deliver us. In whom we trust that He will still deliver us. (2 Corinthians 1:10)

Stone 5: Oh, how great is your goodness, which you have laid up for those who fear you, which you have prepared for those who trust in you in the presence of the sons of men! You shall hide them in the secret place of your presence from the plots of man. You shall keep them secretly in a pavilion from the strife of tongues. (Psalm 31:19–20)

Let us gather our stones today and sharpen our aim at the enemy. Remember that the final bow of the victory came from the giant's weapon.

84

TRIALS AND TESTING, OH MY

Yes, all that fun stuff. Trials, testing, desert times—what's that all about?

Now it came to pass after these things that God tested Abraham, and said to him, "Abraham!" and he said, "Here I am." Then He said, "Take now your son, your only son Isaac, whom you love, and go to the land of Moriah, and offer him there as a burnt offering on one of the mountains of which I shall tell you." (Genesis 22:1–2)

And you shall remember that the Lord your God led you all the way these forty years in the wilderness, to humble you and test you, to know what was in your heart, whether you would keep His commandments or not. (Deuteronomy 8:2)

However, regarding the ambassadors of the princes of Babylon, whom they sent to him to inquire about the wonder that was done in the land, God withdrew from him, in order to test him that He might know all that was in his heart. (2 Chronicles 32:31)

This is what the word has to say about these times.

> My brethren, count it all joy when you fall into various trials, knowing that the testing of our faith produces patience. But let patience have its perfect work, that you may be perfect and complete, lacking nothing. (James 1:2–4)

You might be thinking, *Lord, that word sounds nice and encouraging, but I feel all alone. Where are you?* His word also says in Hebrews 13:5, "Let your conduct be without covetousness: be content with such things as you have. For He Himself has said, 'I will never leave you or forsake you.'"

> I have prayed for you, that your faith should not fail. (Luke 22:32)

He still has our backs in the dark place. So let's hold on. God is doing a work in us to prove us worthy for kingdom work and victory. The best is yet to come. We are destined to grow and bloom in due season. His word is true and available to us to fight the good fight. His word to us is our weapon to use in every battle we face. Let go and let God do His work. He may withdraw for a season, but He will never leave us.

RAISE A HALLELUJAH

Today, words leave me, and my heart is heavy with confusion, frustration, and an inability to understand what is happening around me. The enemy is coming in like a flood to contribute to all of the above. Help, Lord—shed light on my understanding in this dark time. My prayer and intercession before the Lord brought me this song.

Raise a Hallelujah!

By Jonathan Davis Helser, Melissa Helser, Molly Skaggs, Jake Stevens

I raise a hallelujah, in the presence of my enemies.
I raise a hallelujah, louder than the unbelief,
I raise a hallelujah, and my weapon is a melody.
I raise a hallelujah, heaven comes to fight for me.

I'm going to sing, in the middle of the storm.
Louder and louder, you're going to hear my praises roar.
Up from the ashes, hope will arise.
Death is defeated, the King is alive!

I raise a hallelujah, with everything inside of me.
I raise a hallelujah, I will watch the darkness flee.
I raise a hallelujah, in the middle of the mystery.
I raise a hallelujah, fear you lost your hold on me!

I'm going to sing, in the middle of the storm.
Louder and louder, you're going to hear my praises roar.
Up from the ashes, hope will arise.
Death is defeated, the King is alive!

Sing a little louder, sing a little louder, and sing a little louder.

86

THUS SAYETH THE LORD AND GOD SAID

How do we hear from God? I don't hear that still, small voice, even when I sit still before Him. I need answers to decisions. I need answers regarding which path to take. I am confused about this situation before me. We have all uttered those cries and had those thoughts at one time or another. We forget sometimes that those answers lie as close as our Bibles, within reach of our hands. He speaks through His written word; we just have to pick that book up to begin to hear Him speak. *The Moody Handbook of Theology* by Paul P. Enns records that the Bible declares "God said" or "thus says the Lord" thirty-eight hundred times. I'm sure I told my kids to clean up the messes in their rooms about the same number of times. My parents said the same things to me, among other things, as they guided me on my journey of life. I can hear my parents' voices as well as my own: "I have told you a hundred times to _____"—you fill in the blank. God, our Father in heaven, will also tell us what to do and guide us on our journey thirty-eight hundred times.

Let's take a look at some scriptures.

> Now the Lord had said to Abram: "Get out of your country, from your family and from your father's house, to a land that I will show you." (Genesis 12:1)

Then Elisha said, "Hear the word of the Lord." Thus says the Lord:. "Tomorrow about this time a measure of fine flour shall be sold for a shekel, and two seahs of barley for a shekel, at the gate of Samaria." (2 Kings 7:1)

Then the Lord answered Job out of the whirlwind, and said, "Who is this who darkens counsel by words without knowledge? Now prepare yourself like a man. I will question you, and you shall answer me. Where were you when I laid the foundations of the earth? Tell me, if you have understanding." (Job 38:1–4)

"For behold, the day is coming, burning like an oven, and all the proud, yes, all who do wickedly will be stubble. And the day which is coming shall burn them up," says the Lord of hosts. (Malachi 4:1)

When all the people were baptized, it came to pass that Jesus also was baptized, and while He prayed, the heaven was opened and the Holy Spirit descended in bodily form like a dove upon Him, and a voice came from heaven which said, "You are my beloved son; in you I am well pleased." (Luke 3:21–22)

Yes, He speaks. The Bible is full of wisdom and directions. It's not our best friend, our neighbor, our therapy group, or our self-help book; it's the Bible where we find our answers, our rest, and our wisdom. Start your engines—your search engines—and let your next search take you to the Bible.

TROUBLED WATERS

December 2020

After a worldwide pandemic, lockdowns, election issues, and a major snowstorm, Lord, I am weary. Dear Lord, have mercy—my daily prayer. I woke up one morning, and the song I wanted to sing all day was a 1970 classic, "Bridge over Troubled Waters" by Simon and Garfunkel, the song of the year. This song doesn't leave my mind. *Could this be you, Lord, talking to me?* I have learned that persistence is usually the Lord prompting me. So I Googled the lyrics and thought about how appropriate they were. *Are you our bridge over these troubled times?* Now I am looking for a scripture to confirm what I think the message is. This is what I was led to.

> And it came to pass in the twelfth year, in the twelfth month, on the first day of the month, that the word of the Lord came to me, saying, "Son of man, take up a lamentation for Pharaoh king of Egypt, and say to him, 'You are like a young lion among the nations, and you are like a monster in the seas, bursting forth in your rivers, troubling the waters with your feet and fouling the rivers. Thus says the Lord God: I will therefore spread My net over you with a company of many people,

and they will draw you up on the land; I will cast you out on the open fields, and cause to settle on you all the birds of the heavens, and with you I will fill the beasts of the whole earth. I will lay your flesh on the mountains, and fill the valleys with your carcass.'" (Ezekiel 32:1–5)

There were no bridges in that day, but there were plenty of nets. Either way, our God is a help over troubled waters. Be encouraged during this season of troubled waters. We know who stirs them and who can calm them. Sing today.
Bridge Over Troubled Water

When you are weary, feeling small,
When tears are in your eyes, I will dry them all.
I am on your side.
Oh, when times get rough and friends just can't be found,
Like a bridge over troubled water I will lay me down.
Like a bridge over troubled water, I will lay me down.
When you're down and out, when you're on the street,
When evening falls so hard I will comfort you,.
I'll take your part.
When darkness comes and pain is all around,
Like a bridge over troubled water I will lay me down.
Like a bridge over troubled water I will lay me down.

Sail on, silver girl. Sail on by.
Your time has come to shine.
All your dreams are on their way.
See how they shine.

Oh, if you need a friend, I'm sailing right behind.
Like a bridge over troubled water I will ease your mind.
Like a bridge over troubled water I will ease your mind.

88

GOODBYE

As we gather together by video call, teleconference, or a socially distanced gathering, we bid farewell to this year—a year we will never forget and will talk about for years to come. We will read books and see movies about this year that are yet to be produced. Commentaries will be varied according to each writer's perception of events. There is only one thing that is a constant, the word of God. It is a word that doesn't return void. When our foundations are shaking and Satan is on the loose, the only sure weapon is God's glorious promises. Our sword is the word of God for those who put their trust in Him. I share some of those promises.

> As for God, His way is perfect, the word of the Lord is proven. He is a shield to all who trust in Him. (2 Samuel 22:31)

> Oh, how great is your goodness, which you have laid up for those who fear You. Which you have prepared for those who trust in you in the presence of the sons of men! (Psalm 31:19)

Be of good courage, and He shall strengthen your heart, all you who hope in the Lord. (Psalm 31:24)

Commit your way to the Lord, trust also in Him, and He shall bring it to pass. (Psalm 37:5)

Trust in Him at all times, you people, pour out your heart before Him. God is a refuge for us. (Psalm 62:8)

Those who trust in the Lord are like Mount Zion, which cannot be moved, but abides forever. (Psalm 125:1)

Don't give up. Keep standing.

89

ALWAYS A PLAN

It is January 17, 2021, and COVID-19 numbers are spiking after the holidays. Fear and anxiety abound. Political division and a dread of unrest and the return of riots and protests that dominated the streets this summer are prevalent. Confusion is on every front. God help us.

The Lord brought me to 1 Kings 17. I share it with you in the hope that it ministers peace, His peace, to you.

> Get away from here and turn eastward, and hide by the Brook Cherith, which flows into the Jordan. And it shall be that you shall drink from the brook, and I have commanded the ravens to feed you there. (1 Kings 17:3–4)

In this scripture, the Lord warns Elijah of the coming drought and the provision He has made for him.

> Arise, go to Zarephath, which belongs to Sidon, and dwell there. See, I have commanded a widow there to provide for you. (1 Kings 17:9)

This is plan B. Elijah went to the widow's home and found that she had very little to share.

She was preparing the last bit of flour for herself and her son and getting ready to die.

> For thus says the Lord God of Israel: "The bin of flour shall not be used up, nor shall the jar of oil run dry, until the day the Lord sends rain on the earth." (1 Kings 17:14)

It happened that the widow's young child became ill.

> And he said to her, "Give me your son." So he took him out of her arms and carried him to the upper room where he was staying, and laid him on his own bed. Then he cried out to the Lord and said, "O Lord my God, have You also brought tragedy on the widow with whom I lodge, by killing her son?" And he stretched himself out on the child three times, and cried out to the Lord and said, "O Lord my God, I pray, let this child's soul come back to him." (1 Kings 17:19–21)

Yes, the child lived. Elijah was in the right place at the right time. The Lord heard his prayer and provided in every way.

> But God has chosen the foolish things of the word to put to shame the wise, and God has chosen the weak things of the world to put to shame the things which are mighty. And the base things of the world and the things which are despised God has chosen and the things which are not, to bring to nothing the things that are, that no flesh should glory in His presence. (1 Corinthians 1:27–29)

Faithful God, you do have a plan—not of us, but of you that no human may take your glory away. Hallelujah, praise the living God! I love that this word is not only for us but for our households as it was for Zarephath. I pray it brings peace to those who fear and that you find faith in your church.

COME FOLLOW ME

It's been a few months of constant intercession for so many reasons on so many levels. Nothing I see or hear indicates breakthrough. Lost hope and confusion were beginning to set in. Was my intercession in line with what God wanted? Wow—is that doubt setting in too? Don't tell me you haven't been there too. On Sunday morning, I joined my church service online as the snow fell and mounded up outside my window. I praised the Lord, took communion, and listened to the various testimonies that were shared. As the message for the day was being spoken, I felt my spirit quicken, and my ears became attentive to every word that was spoken. God was speaking to me through the speaker and the message he was bringing. His words were giving conformation to my spirit. Was it a long, complicated sermon? No, not particularly. The point that this Sunday morning's message was bringing was about striving. Why do we strive and grow weary? Why do we lose hope and become confused? Because we forget who God is and His power. We forget His character and His heart. I suggest a study and review on the character of God. We all know about it but need the reminder every so often. I felt I got a permission slip from God to sit back and let go and let God—not that I would give up praying, but I would pray differently. I would pray in His will and timing and add that to requests and petitions that I was praying about, leaving it there in His throne room. I pondered this message for the rest of the day and began to feel my spirit lifting. He never leaves us or forsakes us. He wants us to know Him. I will say that again: He wants us to know Him and for us to never forget Him and who He is because He does not forget us.

I have been waking up with words from songs, some secular and some praise tunes, playing in my mind. This is new for me, never having experienced it before. I know some people experience it all the time. This morning I heard, "Come follow me and I will give you rest," words from a song from my past. I loved it then and still do. I searched for the words and found the song—"Be Not Afraid" written by Bob Dufford, a Jesuit priest. It confirmed the sermon I heard this past Sunday. I leave you with the words of the song. May they bless and speak to you also. I also leave you with the scriptures God led me to as I was listening to the song.

> And the Lord, He is the One who goes before you. He will be with you, He will not leave you nor forsake you, do not fear nor be dismayed. (Deuteronomy 31:8)

> A thousand may fall at your side, and ten thousand at your right hand, but none shall not come near you. (Psalm 91:7)

> Come to me, all you who labor and are heavy laden, and I will give you rest. (Matthew 11:28)

Be Not Afraid

You shall cross the barren desert,
but you shall not die of thirst.
You shall wander far in safety
Though you do not know the way.
You shall speak your words in foreign lands
and all will understand.

You shall see the face of God and live.

Be not afraid. I go before you always.
Come follow me and I shall give you rest.

If you pass through raging waters in the sea,
you shall not drown.
If you walk amidst the burning flames,
you shall not be harmed.
If you stand before the power of hell and death is at your side,
Know that I am with you through it all.

Be not afraid. I go before you always.
Come follow me and I shall give you rest.

Amen.

91

HOPE

How does one go on without hope? We do not—we die, in body and spirit. Why is it different for believers? We have the word of God, which gives us the hope we need to go on. Let's look at some of those scriptures.

> Be of good courage, and he shall strengthen your heart, all you who hope in the Lord. (Psalm 31:24)

> Why are you cast down, O my soul? And why are you disquieted within me. Hope in God, for I shall yet praise Him for the help of His countenance. (Psalm 42:5)

> Thus says the Lord: "A voice was heard in Ramah, Lamentation and bitter weeping, Rachel weeping for her children, refusing to be comforted for her children, because they were no more." Thus says the Lord: "Refrain your voice from weeping, and your eyes from tears. For your work shall be rewarded, and they shall come back from the land of the enemy. There is hope in your future, says the Lord that

your children shall come back to their own border."
(Jeremiah 31:15–17)

Who, contrary to hope, in hope believed, so that he
became the father of many nations, according to what
was spoken, "So shall your descendants be." (Romans
4:18)

Therefore gird up the loins of your mind, be sober, and
rest your hope fully upon the grace that is to be brought
to you at the revelation of Jesus Christ. (1 Peter 1:13)

Let us not forget the word of God in our hopelessness. It is available literally at our fingertips. Just open the Bible in times of despair. God is waiting to speak encouragement and give us hope. Simple as that. It is a basket filled with berries.

92

HOPE AGAIN

As the fear and anxiety of the pandemic mount on us, we need more hope. The virus, the political division, the rising gas and food prices, the bombing in Syria and the rumors of war—it's too much. What have you to say, my Lord?

> But those who wait on the Lord shall renew their strength. They shall mount up with wings like eagles. They shall run and not be weary. They shall walk and not faint. (Isaiah 40:31)

> For I know the plans and thoughts that I think toward you, says the Lord, thoughts of peace

> And not of evil, to give you a future and a hope. (Jeremiah 29:11)

> You are my hiding place and my shield. I hope in your word. (Psalm 119:114)

> Now may the God of hope fill you with all joy and peace in believing that you

may abound in hope by the power of the Holy Spirit (Romans 15:13)

… the eyes of your understanding being enlightened; that you may know what is the hope of His calling, what are the riches of the glory of His inheritance in the saints. (Ephesians 1:18)

Therefore gird up the loins of your mind, be sober, and rest your hope fully upon the grace that is to be brought to you at the revelation of Jesus Christ. (1 Peter 1:13)

Be blessed today with hope from the very words of our Lord and our Savior. I end this book with the words of a song that I woke up to this morning, "Because He Lives" by Bill and Gloria Gaither.

Because He lives, I can face tomorrow.
Because He lives all fear is gone.
Because I know He holds the future
And life is worth living just because He lives.

God bless you and yours today and always. May your life be filled with berries.

About the Author

The author shares her postings from a blog that she created after her book titled Take My Hand and Walk With Me was published. The book created many questions from her readers, and the blog was a way of communicating with them. She shares the different ways God speaks to us. Her hope is that you will learn how to recognize this heavenly communication. She refers to these random encounters as berries, small sweet things that can give your spirit a boost. She has experienced much of life as a nurse, missionary, mother, grandmother mentor, and author. She has learned that there is light after the darkness, and there is a God that wants to speak to us. He speaks from His word, in dreams, and everyday random actions, and thoughts. It is this author's prayer that we listen and hear to what God is speaking to us.

Printed in the United States
by Baker & Taylor Publisher Services